UNCOILING

a memoir
of anxiety,
aneurysm and
renewal

_____

To Stan
love Judith

Judith Marcus

Most names have been changed to protect privacy;
some chronology of events have been altered to allow
the story to flow; and to those of you who wanted names
and events to be as they are: thank you!

Print Edition ISBN: 978-0-9856998-0-2
EPUB Edition ISBN: 978-0-9856998-1-9
MOBI Edition ISBN: 978-0-9856998-2-6

Library of Congress Control Number: 2012941872

Cover Art by Robin Pederson
Illustration by Robert Williamson
All photos are from Judith's personal collection

Kousa Press
Seattle, Washington

to my mother, Muriel

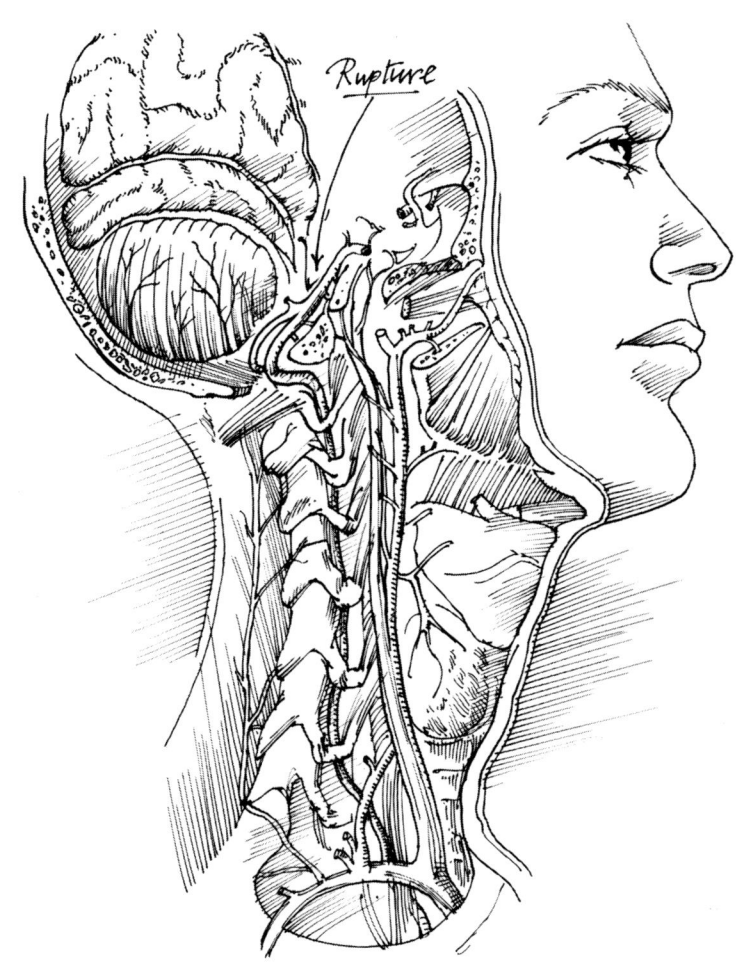
Rupture

CONTENTS

PART
ONE

Seeing Red

Blood is the carrier of the soul.

JO EVANS

"JUST RETURN TO your life as if nothing happened," he said, and I looked straight ahead, taking in nothing, seeing only the red. Speckles of red blood had embedded themselves in the back of my eyes, veiling everything I saw in a rose-colored reminder of the grave injuries I'd suffered. The neurosurgeon continued to speak reassuringly, but I sat stunned and uncomprehending, while my husband nodded compliantly, somberly taking in the information I was not yet able to comprehend.

"As if nothing happened," the surgeon had said, just days after my brain had exploded, days after he had cut into my leg, plunged his microscopic instruments deep into my femoral artery, snaking a titanium filament through the arterial system, up the length of my body to the back of my brain. There, he tightly knotted the metal into a coil, woven like a tiny bird's nest to force my blood to reroute and find a new and different pathway to the tissues of my brain.

Something *had* happened, I thought. Each fragment of word, idea, and sensation that passed through my new and reborn brain, danced across my neurons so delicately that I could nearly feel their butterfly weight inside my skull. *So this is what it is to remember,* I thought, *this is what it is for the body to memorize its own transforming story.*

I was one of the rare lucky ones, the neurosurgeon repeated, as if to remind me that what had happened to me had been cause for celebration. The aneurysm may not have left my body paralyzed, may not have left me speechless nor my brain disarticulated into bits and pieces, but I knew intuitively that it had left my body damaged in complex yet unseen ways.

As a longtime CranioSacral therapist specializing in soft tissue manipulation and somatic work, I understood that the body has much to teach. What might my "lucky" body and brain teach me, I wondered? Could this aneurysm which left me seemingly whole and unchanged, teach my mind and body lessons in healing that I would not have otherwise discovered? Could the trauma that so terrified me and my family have been a gift of grace, a blessing that I would come to understand in time? I now still feared it in the way one fears an uninvited stranger walking through the door into one's most sacred home.

The aneurysm hit like a tidal wave and left me standing on the shores of my own past. Just months before I had been struggling with a torment of anxiety so great that it had left me shaking on the ground, medicating my mind and body into compliance so that I could successfully maintain my work as a somatic therapist.

For over two decades I had studied and worked with people's bodies, had held the heads of others in my trained hands, freeing fascia and neurological patterns through which the mind and body communicate. Now I wondered if I could continue in my life's work. Had my own mind and body become so damaged by a vague and persistent state of panic that I could no longer help my clients? I once was certain of my skills and gifts, but in the months before the injury to my brain, a mounting uncertainty had taken hold. My doubts had so battered me that I questioned everything I'd learned and everything I'd known about my own abilities.

Suddenly, one morning I had awoken trembling, panting and whispering vague and indiscernible words as if I were possessed. And I was possessed; possessed by an intruding stranger—a blood clot that occluded my brain, only to abandon me with a peculiar nonchalance, as if just passing through.

The aneurysm left me with no visible injuries, just trace evidence in my eyes to mark the trauma I'd endured. *What might I discover*, I wondered, *if I pursue this trace evidence through my own body and its memories?* Might I rediscover my own gift for healing by tracking the trail that the broken blood vessel had inscribed across my body and across the years? Could I unravel the mysteries of my flesh and bones like a forensic scientist to discern the stories they might tell?

This is the story of my journey from healer to healed, as I reflect on my career as a somatic therapist, and the explosion in my brain that revolutionized my life and work.

Childhood

Save your strength
to swim with the tide.

DANNA FAULDS

I WAS BORN into the atomic age, coming into the world on the front-lines of the Baby Boom in 1951, unaware and unprepared for what lay ahead. World War II had come to an end and the Korean War was just beginning. The Russians had tested their first atomic bomb, and the Cold War was heating up. Suburban homes were filled with new appliances and instant foods, and homeowners escaped to the cheerful lure of that new magical box, the television. Technology was transforming lives, and society was desperate to race into the future. There was no better time to be born, and no worse time to leave the comfortable cradle of my mother's womb.

The soft walls that held me hardened and constricted, again and again with increasing force. Then all was quiet. Terror engulfed me as I fought to hold myself in place. I did not want to be uncurled and squeezed through the tight space that pulled me toward the noise and glaring lights ahead. I held back, I resisted, refusing to be born.

The cold, hard steel of the forceps pushed my mother's vaginal walls wide open, but she didn't make a sound. She could not cry out, could not scream as her body was leveraged open. She had been medicated "the modern way," which is to say into unconscious compliance, and my own small brain and tiny body were deadened by the drugs, as well. The metal forceps were clamped onto my head, and I was pulled and twisted through my mother's vagina, as if I were being swallowed alive by a ravenous snake, to be digested by the world.

I was born screaming, held upside down and then brought to rest down the hall from my sleeping mother. My father, hating the sight of blood, had waited outside the hospital. Thus their firstborn girl arrived onto the earth.

—

I suckled a rubber nipple and drank artificial mother's milk, a sweet concoction sold to women as a modern wonder food for their newborn infants. I slept alone in a large crib, and I played alone in an even larger playpen, caged for my own safety. I gazed at the bright design of the green and white quilt that covered me when I was put in my bed to sleep and it became my map to a world of my imaginings, its geometric shapes turning to pathways and structures that I alone could discern and navigate.

When my mother took me outdoors, I was placed inside an enormous baby carriage that she pushed along the sidewalk; I could not see her distant smile of pride. My eyes were protected from the sun by the dark navy blue hood of the carriage, as if I'd been placed inside a box and sealed away. I heard only her familiar steps, so far from my small body. When the ride came to a stop, she picked me up, pulled me to her face and kissed me.

My mother never talked about my birth, nor did my father. It was an irrelevant topic in those days. Like any child, I felt my existence to have been without beginning. I simply was. Had always been. Would always be. I *was* my thoughts, just as I was my changing body, the body that learned to stand, to walk, to run, to fall, to climb, to grasp, to tie a shoe.

My body intrigued me, delighted me, as I discovered its rapidly changing contours. My hair grew, curled and coiled, was cut, and grew in curls and coils still again. I loved to have it brushed, the gentle tug of the hair brush massaging my scalp, soothing me.

—

My flesh tickled when it was touched in certain places. The base of my feet, under my skinny arms, and along the sides of my ribs. My body twisted and squirmed in delight at my father's touch, making me laugh without control. But when my ribs were held tightly in my mother's arms, they did not tickle. They felt safe, secure, tightly fastened to my spine. I nestled into my mother's embrace and wished she'd never let me go. As I grew older, and my baby sisters came, she no longer had the time to hold me that way.

When my skin was very cold, it puckered into a thousand tiny bumps like chicken flesh, and my spine quivered, forcing me to hug myself for warmth. When my skin grew hot with fever, I felt the heat seep into my tissues, cooking me until I cried for my mother to cool me with a cold cloth soaked in soothing water. When my skin erupted into big, red splotches and bumps that itched miserably, my body tormented me with unrelenting pain. The body that had intrigued me betrayed me. I cried to have my body back, to be me again, to live at peace inside my flesh and bones that moved in rhythm to my breathing.

The world around me kept changing and I discovered my clothes shrinking until they were too small, my shoes too tight, the legs of chairs and tables becoming shorter just as my parents' arms grew closer to my up-turned face until they could easily touch my head when I stood before them. I loved to have my head touched and soothed; it brought me immense relief, though at that time I did not know from what. I knew only that my head so often hurt, for no reason, as if I needed to remember something.

"Run along," they'd say, pushing me away with their large hands, "Children should be seen and not heard."

"Go play now."

"You're getting too big to be picked up, that's for babies."

I watched my mother pick up my baby sister, place her in the playpen and walk away.

She gave me chocolate chip cookies and milk, after we had baked them together.

If I concentrated hard enough, with all my might, I could feel my bones lengthen and expand, my muscles tighten, my skin stretch into its new evolving shape.

But I told no one.

My body was my secret home.

My own hands its secret key.

—

I grew up about twenty miles north of New York City in Westchester County, New York. Although the white settlement in Westchester dated back to the Revolutionary War, and the region was known for its old money wealth, new money was pouring in. As highways were laid connecting the community to the city, the world's first large-scale suburban area was born, and soon corporations like IBM and Pepsi established their headquarters at our doorstep. This served our family well. My father was a real estate mortgage investor and he prospered with the growth of the suburbs. He took the commuter train to Manhattan every day, where money was made with the speed of an introduction and a lunch of two or three martinis.

My mother dreamed of a life in fashion design. She had taken classes at Drexel Institute in Philadelphia, but it would be years before she had a career of her own outside the home. She adapted to her role as a post-war wife and mother with grace, as if she had no other desires. She dressed stylishly, socialized day and night, and went shopping. Sometimes she brought me along with her, and made me try on stiff, itchy dresses that scratched my body and kept me from moving like the neighborhood boys I liked to play with. I could not climb in the dresses, or run in the stiff patent-leather shoes. The petticoats beneath the dresses made my skin hot and sticky. I begged for overalls, and she would sometimes indulge me. Eventually, I begged not to go shopping, and before long she stopped taking me along.

When the stores offered something new called "Charge and Send," big rectangular boxes began to arrive in the mail. Boxes filled with velvet and taffeta dresses, hot, confining tights with crotches that slipped nearly to my knees and little gloves with pearly buttons arrived in the mail soon after my mother's shopping trips. She loved the dresses she had chosen for me and made me try them on.

"Come on, Judy, hold still, I want to see you in this beautiful dress. Now isn't this pretty? Don't you love this big bow in the front?"

I squirmed inside the dresses and my mother's voice grew sharp. "Hold still! Don't you want to look pretty? Don't you want Daddy to see how pretty you look in your new dress? Do you have any idea how much this dress cost?"

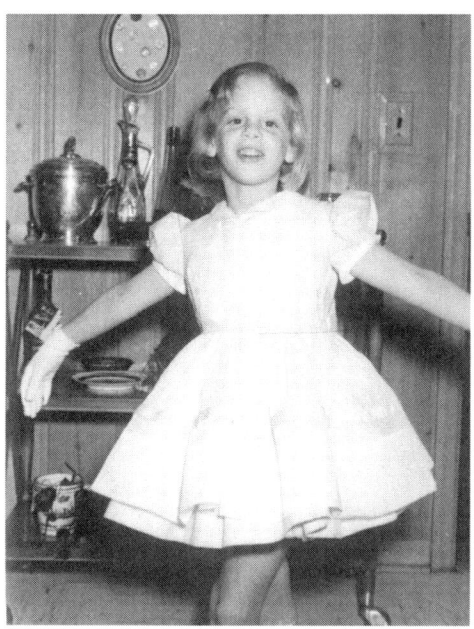

I wanted to run outside and play. The maple leaves had fallen and been raked into big red and orange piles, like mountains to be climbed.

I would climb the maple leaf mountain and declare myself the ruler.

As soon as I could get out of the pretty dresses and join the boys outside.

———

There weren't many girls in our neighborhood, so I grew up mostly playing with the boys. But they always reminded me I was *a girl*, which meant I was somehow defective. They really liked playing with me, but they didn't expect me to be as strong or as brave or as smart as they were.

When we played war games, I was the nurse, and they were the heroes. When we played cowboys and Indians, I was the one who was kidnapped and tied to a tree, waiting to be rescued. When we played cops and robbers, I was the screaming victim, and they were the ones with power. I accepted my submissive roles for the most part, because being a girl meant seeing myself as they saw me; I had a different body, so I was different. Sometimes that was a good thing; I loved being the nurse, because I liked taking care of people. Other times it was lonely, because I did not like waiting to be rescued.

It became very important for me to prove myself to my friends, to show them that I did have strength and courage, that I was just as capable as they were. I climbed higher, I ran faster, I took more chances.

One blistering cold winter day, a pond by our house had frozen solid. We would skate and slide around on the rim of the pond, slipping and sliding and enjoying ourselves immensely. But we knew that the ice grew thinner toward the center, where it was deepest, and going too far out on a frozen body of water was dangerous.

But I thought it was probably safe enough to explore. I could see many small trees poking up from the ice; if I began to fall, I could grab onto one and pull myself to safety. The temperature had dropped so low that we could see our breath and our fingers grew numb within minutes; the center of the pond must have been frozen solid. Still, the boys were chicken.

"I dare you to go out there!" they challenged each other, pushing and knocking each other down in a show of bravado.

"Oh, yeah? Well I dare you to eat yellow snow!"

Inevitably, the dares would lead to wrestling each other to the ground in order to avoid responding to the challenge.

I saw an opportunity and took a chance. I slid further and further out on the pond, skating on the soles of my rubber boots, nearly falling. Pretty soon the boys stopped their rough housing and watched from the edge of the pond.

"Judy's crazy!"

"I'll bet she can do it! Go, Judy, Go!"

"Judy, come back, you're going too far, the ice is too thin out there!"

"She can do it!"

"You're going to get in trouble!"

The bitter cold on my face was exhilarating! It stung and hurt and my bones were throbbing from the freezing cold, but I felt like an Olympic skater being cheered to the finish line! No one could call me chicken now!

The cracking of the ice drowned their distant cheers, a sound that only I could hear, alone out there on the pond. It sounded thunderous, as if the world were slowly opening beneath my feet and there was nothing I could do to stop it. In an instant, I plunged through the sharp edges of the ice and into the numbing waters below, the waters swallowed me, as if I were returning to the amniotic waters turned freezing cold.

I pulled myself out as the boys rushed to the edges of the ice to help me to safety. When I got home, shivering and frozen from the cold, my mother stripped off my clothes, put me in a warm bath and then rubbed me up and down with a thick towel, wrapping me up tightly and holding me close to her until I was warmed. I put on my robe and slippers and she made me hot cocoa. Nothing had ever tasted so good, each hot sip slid down my throat like a magical elixir.

I had survived and I'd proven myself to the boys.

—

My father always wanted a son, but instead he had three daughters.

He called us "fellas" and being the oldest, I sometimes got to go with him to football and baseball games and other adventures that were for just us two. He'd act just like a kid, playing and joking around; everything was a party.

"Come on fellas," Other times he'd say to me and my little sisters, "Let's get some ice cream!" Or even better, "Let's go to the circus!"

We loved our special trips and adventures with our dad, but most of the time he was very distant, lost in thought about his work, coming home late from the office when we were all ready for bed, leaving on weekends to play golf. When he was home, he watched sports on t.v., and we weren't supposed to interrupt him. He wasn't much of a talker.

We were not a religious family, but our religion shaped me. We were Jewish, and the social ladder had few rungs for Jewish people in the 1960s, marking us as different from the norm.

One day in school there was an assembly and we were told to rise and say the Lord's Prayer. I panicked, because I didn't even know what the Lord's Prayer was, let alone how to say it. I mumbled along to escape notice, but I realized something was wrong. I was different from my classmates and I wasn't sure what that meant or why. But I knew it had something to do with being Jewish. I studied myself in the mirror for signs of this difference inscribed on my young face, and feared my body would betray me to my classmates. Could they see the hidden history that had been carved into my bones?

"It's nothing to be ashamed of," my mother explained to me about our heritage, as if she were talking about a less than perfect facial feature. It was just what we were, perhaps not what we would have chosen, just something one did not draw attention to. Like a small flaw, really. Nothing to be ashamed of.

In seventh grade my parents told me and my sisters that we would be moving to nearby Scarsdale, New York the following week. I would be leaving my friends and our home, and moving to a new town, where my parents had bought a new home, a home I'd never seen. I was terrified of leaving and refused to leave, clung to my bed as if it could hold me in place. I cried and cried, shook uncontrollably, feeling my body tremble, my spine contract as I curled into a shaking ball of opposition. My head throbbed and tightened as if caught in a vice. But still the movers came, and I was forced to follow.

Scarsdale had originally been unkind to Jews. When a Jewish man who had converted to Christianity tried to escort a Christian woman to the country club in 1961, he was turned away and the club announced that Jewish people were not welcome. A priest from the Church of St. James responded by refusing Holy Communion to any supporters of the club, and people softened. I didn't know anything about this history, though; I just knew that my parents were thrilled to move to Scarsdale for the educational opportunities, and to move up the social ladder. We arrived in the wake of the town's repentance, when Jews were settling throughout the town. We joined the local synagogue, and attended the all-Jewish country club in a nearby town.

We were at the country club one afternoon when I was running around with my cousins, having fun. I was barefoot and I stepped onto the blazing hot blacktop and a jolt of what felt like some kind of electricity shot through the bottom of my foot and up my leg. I felt my pelvis shiver with an incandescent energy like nothing I'd ever felt before. It felt wonderful, but also somehow secret.

I ran back to my cousins feeling like I'd discovered something about my body that I didn't dare reveal.

———

I adjusted to my new life in Scarsdale and soon found the move exciting. Our new home was large and glamorous, the school was far better, and I made many new friends. My mother kept many of her friends as they lived nearby, and still is in contact with some of them today. And although she had three young daughters, she wasn't overwhelmed. Like all wives of successful men back then, she had help.

A series of black maids cleaned and cooked and ironed and watched us, while my mother socialized. Whenever one would leave, another one was hired. They were always black, and usually very sweet. They hugged me, and gave me treats. They lived with us, sleeping in a small room near the kitchen, which we called "the maid's room."

———

One time, shortly after I'd gotten my driver's license, Janey, a long-time maid who I loved, asked me to drive her home on her day off. We always gave the maids one day off each week. So when Janey asked me to take her to her home, I was really surprised. It had never occurred to me that a maid would have her own home nearby. I drove her to her apartment, and I was startled to see that she had an entirely separate life that didn't include us. When we reached her home, she kindly invited me inside.

I began to think about our maids having lives outside our own. It was like discovering Janey's secret, and it made a big impression on me

at the time. I had read James Baldwin's *Notes of a Native Son,* and *The Autobiography of Malcolm X,* (and soon I would read *Soul on Ice* by Eldridge Cleaver, which was published shortly before I graduated from high school in 1969). But these were books by and about Black men. They told me nothing about the world of Black women. Although the civil rights movement was having an enormous impact on the way that young people viewed society, the legacy of slavery and Jim Crow laws had influenced my life in subtle and unseen ways. I had never considered Janey's personal life. Coming face to face with her private life as I stepped into her home, I began to think long and hard about the meaning of racial differences.

I was coming to realize that society was organized around our ideas about body image, about body shape, skin color and genetic ancestry. The result of reacting to body images and differences could increase hatred and start wars. Could this same power be directed toward something constructive? My understanding at that point remained a blur; I would later enter graduate school and study these issues more deeply. At this time, in my high school years, my focus on the human body was under the power of my hormones. And I was thrilled to discover that my own body brought me a new awareness of myself and boys.

I'd begun dating early, at about the age of fourteen. It was 1965, the era of free love. We were the first generation coming of age with access to birth control, which meant that sex didn't have to lead to marriage or parenting until we wanted it to. Of course, I wasn't ready for actual intercourse, but the pungent scent of hormones drives any teenager into a state of physical delirium and confusing desires. The boys I'd once played with were growing into men, and I into a woman. It was only natural that I'd find my tomboy ways turning into tomcat ways as I pursued my own sexual discoveries, one step at a time, in the arms of teenage boys.

My mother promptly got me on birth control pills, but not without a stern warning that I'd better never need them.

"Just because I'm getting these for you doesn't mean you can start tramping around. Your father and I only want what's best for you and if you get pregnant, you'll lose your reputation. And there's nothing more valuable than a girl's reputation, do you hear me? Nothing! Now, here, keep these pills someplace where people won't see them. And don't tell your father!"

I nodded compliantly and took them, although I knew I didn't need them. I *loved* heavy petting, but I was in no way ready to go any further than that. My body belonged to me.

Still, as desirable as my body was to some boys, and as powerful as it was coming to feel to me; to my parents, it was an object that needed improving. My body just wasn't good enough to meet their standards.

"You're going to need to lose weight if you ever want a husband," my mother would say, pointing out how tight my jeans were or how I didn't need that extra helping of potatoes. "If you keep eating those big bowls of ice cream, you're going to be sorry," my dad would say sternly. Our childhood days of slipping out for ice cream had come to an end. Now such spontaneous actions were something to be ashamed of and anxious about.

As my adolescent body began developing, my parents worried I was gaining too much weight. Perceiving my curves as fat, they began sending me to doctors for diet pills and lectures, a common practice of that time. While I'd been born in the era of Marilyn Monroe—whose curves and figure were considered the hallmark of female beauty—by the time I became a teenager the supermodel "Twiggy" was an international phenomenon, and her androgynous adolescent physique became the new image of women's beauty.

"These will help curb that appetite of yours," the doctor said as he prescribed me amphetamine pills, "and you'll have a lot more energy!" I thought it was pretty weird that my parents were so worried that I not get involved in the "drug culture," while they were sending me to the doctors for "speed" just so I could fit into a size six. But I wanted my parents to stop bothering me, and I wanted my body to be acceptable to them, so I took the pills. Looking back on this now, I can see that my nervous system was being molded towards anxiety from the effect of these medications.

After awhile, they made me go to the doctor by myself. I remember taking the train to the city to see the diet doctors, feeling so humiliated riding alone on that commuter train, heading to New York City to get pills to make me look right. Once I got there, I had to step onto the scale for the weigh in—my body was weighed and evaluated by strangers who would either praise or scold me depending on how far to the right they had to move the scale weight. No matter how it turned out, I felt as if there were something fundamentally wrong with me and my body.

I also knew that no matter what my size or shape, my parents were very proud of me as their first-born daughter grew up. Still, the scrutiny over my body and any caustic remarks had left scars. It made me very aware of how much my body and my worth were so closely tied, of how much I was evaluated by society in terms of the shape of my body and not my own nature.

I don't know to what extent that awareness influenced my path to healing, but it did spark a dawning awareness that sufferings are inscribed on our bodies. My body became evidence of the anxiety that was slowly taking root inside me, first through the weight that I put on as I ate to soothe my nerves, later as I took pills to try to fit into the framework of social approval. I did my best to get through high school. I couldn't wait to leave home for college.

Go West,
Young Woman,
Go West

It seemed like a matter of minutes
(when we) saw stretched out ahead of us
the fabulous white city of San Francisco
on her eleven mystic hills with the
blue Pacific and its advancing wall of
potato-patch fog beyond...

JACK KEROUAC

IN MY SENIOR year of high school, it came time to choose a university. My grades were high and my parents well off so I had a number of choices, but they wanted me close to home. I was excited about the prospect of going to Brandeis University in Massachusetts, and they liked the idea of me going to a university with a strong Jewish heritage. Although religion had never been very important to us, they were disappointed that I wasn't dating many Jewish boys, and they thought that might change if I attended Brandeis.

But once we visited the campus, my hopes for going there were dashed. There were too many hippies there, my parents declared, so they sent me instead to the less radical Syracuse University in New York. It didn't matter, really, for the Vietnam war protests and drugs were everywhere. That's when my period of rebellion from my roots really began.

Once I got to Syracuse, I was drawn into a world of art. My love of art had been kindled in high school, when I got involved in extracurricular activities for the yearbook. I loved learning about painting and photography, and once I realized how creative I could be, I took private art classes from a bohemian artist who travelled weekly from Greenwich Village to the suburbs to teach. By the time I got to Syracuse University, the artist inside me was ready to be born.

The campus was a mosaic of architectural history with buildings reflecting Romanesque to modern styles, and beautiful sculptures lined the walkways. Classes in art and religion particularly fascinated me, and began to draw me out of the insulated world I'd been living in. They awakened a spirit inside me that I hadn't even realized lay dormant. A vibrant world of color and form opened itself to me in college and I was fascinated.

In high school, I had begun to put together a small portfolio, but now in college, I began to draw frantically, filling journals and sketchbooks with spontaneous visions that appeared on the page as if by magic. Writhing, sinewy bodies and torsos, blossoming vaginas and serpentine penises filled my pages, alongside twisting trees and spiraled limbs, smooth, rounded rocks and primordial shells. The images emerged from me as if they were splinters of my many selves that I barely knew existed, a fusion of flesh and nature that helped me to realize that my body was a part of the earth. It was filled with volcanic emotions. Although I didn't know what I was doing back then, I would hike in the fields and woods to ground myself. I liked to imagine I was feeling my body's roots going into the earth like an ancient tree.

However the university was hardly fertile ground for the growth of my spirit, and by the end of my second year at Syracuse, I was done with it. My girlfriend and I got in a car and drove to California where everything was happening.

We settled in the Bay Area and I called my parents, telling them that I would not be coming back. They were shocked, furious, worried and annoyed, but there was nothing they could say to persuade me to return. Resigned to my decision, they asked only that I finish my education, if not at Syracuse, then in a school in California. I moved into a commune in Berkeley, enrolled in the San Francisco Art Institute, and pursued a Bachelor's degree in Fine Arts.

Those were pretty wild times, and I was smack dab in the center of the whole hippie scene. The people, the parties, the protests—it was an endless psychedelic adventure. I was most enthralled with the natural world that surrounded me. The Sierra Nevada mountains were so majestic compared to the Adirondacks in upstate New York. I felt most alive when I hiked and inhaled the cool, thin air of these granite geologic wonders. I spent as much time in nature as I possibly could: walking, hiking, camping. It was a very rich time, carving out a life of my own away from my parents. I realized how much I had just never fit into East coast culture; on the West coast, everything was more casual and friendly, and I fit right in. I made many friends and had a steady boyfriend; he even wanted to marry me, but I wasn't ready.

By the time I graduated in 1973 with my B.F.A. degree and a teaching certificate, I had another steady boyfriend. He was moving to Oregon to go to graduate school in biochemistry in Corvallis, and the thought of living in distant rural Oregon in the seventies sounded very exotic. More importantly, living in the country felt right to my body. The back to the land movement was at its peak, and I longed to be a part of it—to grow our own vegetables and live close to nature. So we moved to Oregon in 1975 and I got a job as a Kindergarten teacher with an alternative school. I loved teaching and the children; I loved inspiring children to learn and to think in new and more creative ways, but it never really felt like I was where I was permanently meant to be. I enjoyed the work and the children, but I knew deep down that I hadn't really found my purpose. The longer my boyfriend was in graduate school, the more I realized that the life of a lab wife was not for me. We slowly drifted apart, and eventually, broke up. It wasn't long before I found a new boyfriend, and we moved in together outside of Corvallis where we lived a rural lifestyle, growing our own food, chopping our own wood, swimming naked in the rivers in the summer, and walking endlessly by the sea in the winter.

One winter I started having back pain. Since I chopped a lot of wood for the wood stove, I just assumed it was the result of tired, sore muscles. However the pain kept getting worse, so I was forced to start paying attention, because it was increasingly clear that it wasn't from sore muscles. The more I focused on the pain, the more I realized that the pain was very deep inside me, and then I realized it could be my spine which I'd never really thought much about before. Like most people, until the pain began I'd taken my spine for granted, never feeling the bend of my neck, the twist of my back, the movement of each vertebral disc. It took searing pain for me to see that even though I thought I knew about my own body, I'd been oblivious to to many things about it. Why was it hurting so?

I happened to know an orthopedic surgeon at the time, so I consulted him about the pain.

"You're going to need surgery," he said, matter-of-factly, "or I could prescribe some medication, but you'd have to take it the rest of your life."

His dire diagnosis was hardly what I wanted to hear, much less what I was going to accept just because he'd said it. I was 29 at the time, and had many years ahead of me and I wasn't about to spend it hooked on pain medication. Nor was I about to go under the knife; the thought of someone cutting into my spinal column simply terrified me. I knew there had to be another answer.

"No thank you," I said, in a moment of grace, refusing his state of the art conventional medical treatment, "I'll call you if I need you." I left, determined to figure something else out.

In the meantime, my boyfriend had been going to a chiropractor for his back pain. I didn't know anything about chiropractic treatment back then. It seemed to be helping him, so when he suggested I give it a try, I agreed. The chiropractor X-rayed my spine and put me on a regimen of exercises. He suggested yoga, fasting and a better diet, but I couldn't really see how my diet related to my spine. I thought it sounded cool however, and we already shopped for our groceries at a nearby co-op where local, organic foods were abundant. So I began going to him regularly for treatments, ate better food and took up yoga.

I'd been meditating and studying Zen Buddhism during that time, and was very intrigued with anything Japanese. I found the two forms of bodywork, yoga and chiropractic treatment, to be compatible with buddhist meditation. I felt centered and calmed afterward, and in turn, my back felt better.

I began focusing on my breath and my body's ability to move. Soon afterward, I was introduced to a woman who taught movement classes according to something called the Feldenkrais Method. She explained that the Feldenkrais Method would increase my body awareness and comfort, and that sounded like precisely the sort of thing I was looking for both as a patient who was in pain and as a budding student of body/mind awareness. I enrolled in her classes, with no idea what would happen.

The class was rather uneventful at first, even anti-climatic. I was all psyched for something radical and exciting, but instead, she just had us lie on the hard carpeted floor, with no cushion, and feel the sensation of our bodies pressed against the hard surface. When we were instructed to move, the movements were so minimal that they were barely discernible. Sometimes the movement was so slow and uneventful that I would find myself drifting off to sleep as I listened to my own breath whispering through my nostrils. I thought to myself, "What's this all about?" It was relaxing, but I had no idea how it could possibly help my back.

But by the end of that first class, I got up off the floor, thinking nothing much had happened, only to realize that my back pain was gone! It was miraculous; nothing had ever eliminated it entirely before, but whatever we were doing, it was working. I was curious and excited, and knew then that I was going to become a Feldenkrais Practitioner.

I began going regularly to the classes, called "Awareness Through

Movement," and it wasn't long before I realized that far from doing nothing, we were meditating in motion! The simple body movements she had us doing made me aware of parts of my body that I had never even known I could access. I found the work fascinating, and saw almost immediately how much it aligned with my interests in mind and awareness; I had to learn more.

Meanwhile my relationship with my boyfriend had become stagnant. He was very depressed and his behavior was so erratic that I was becoming terribly anxious myself. I had no idea what was wrong with me that was making him so unhappy, or what was wrong with him that was making him so moody, or why our relationship was going nowhere. I didn't know what to do, and the tension between us was only worsening. I even thought maybe we should get married and have kids as the next logical step for us. Fortunately, Sarah, a good friend, advised me against marrying to fix a bad relationship and so, not having much of an understanding about counseling or therapy back then, I decided if I couldn't save him, I could at least save myself. So I packed up and left everything, my boyfriend, my job and the Oregon I loved, and I moved back to California to start a four-year training program in the Feldenkrais Method and pursue a Master's Degree in Somatic Psychology at Antioch University in San Francisco* —a city that was fast becoming the cultural hub of somatic studies, bodywork, and alternative psychotherapy.

—

I realized that if I was going to be a practitioner of the Feldenkrais Method, I would need to develop my counseling skills. One thing I was coming to realize was that the body and mind influence each other and treating the body includes treating the mind. In other words I would change myself, my whole self. This program was just what I needed to

---

* This program is now at California Institute of Integral Studies In San Francisco(CIIS)

interweave these two interests. But that program wouldn't start until fall and the Feldenkrais training was a summer program; so I would begin with movement and the body.

Movement is Life

A gesture is a doorway to a memory.

CATHERINE ADACHI

I MOVED BACK to San Francisco in 1984. It had been seven years since I'd left the Bay Area, and returning felt like coming home. The anxiety that had been building in Oregon as I struggled to make something of my relationship with my boyfriend subsided almost immediately once I found myself back in the crisp, clean air of the Bay Area. Although I'd been living in a fairly rural area in Oregon, I somehow felt more connected to the earth once I was back in San Francisco—perhaps it was the social scene or the breathtaking beauty of the urban landscape cradled by the mountains and sea that felt so calming, like yin and yang balanced once again. It was just what I needed to find my center and gain the awareness I would need for training in bodywork. But it would not come easily.

The Feldenkrais Professional Training Program was housed in a gymnasium in a big wooden building. The building didn't have any insulation, and in the mornings when the fog would roll in it could be very cold, so we brought blankets to keep warm. But by afternoon it was stifling hot. There was no air conditioning, so once the fog lifted it wasn't long before we were soaked in sweat. Thankfully, there was a big swimming pool outside so during breaks we took advantage of it and cooled off by jumping in. It could be very uncomfortable either way, but the extremes from bone chilling cold to blood boiling hot only heightened our awareness and helped us to put into practice the techniques we were learning for full body awareness.

—

Moshé Feldenkrais was a remarkable man with an incomparable life story. He was born in 1904 in what is today known as Ukraine. When he was 14 years old he fled to Palestine, bringing with him only a trunk full of what he mischievously called "the finest physics books" that he claimed he had already read. These books were actually the Talmud, the Jewish book of law. By early adulthood, Feldenkrais became a member of the resistance movement to create the free state of Israel. He studied the Japanese self-defense method of Ju-Jitsu that emphasizes awareness of one's own body as well as the opponent's body. Improvising and incorporating his own movement ideas into traditional Ju-Jitsu, he became a skilled fighter and before long he was teaching the resistance fighters how to act and react more effectively.

Despite his political interests, Feldenkrais had no intentions of spending his life fighting; like a true martial artist, he was a man of peace, and eventually he left the resistance movement to pursue scientific studies in France, where he trained under Madame Curie and her husband, the Noble laureate Frédéric Jolie-Curie, receiving his doctorate from the Sorbonne in engineering and physics.

While in France, he had the opportunity to meet Jigaro Kano, the founder of Judo, and presented a manual with his ideas to the master who acknowledged his skillful insights to the art of Judo, an outgrowth of Ju-Jitsu.

When the Nazis invaded France, Feldenkrais fled his home again, this time carrying his suitcase filled with a jar of "heavy water" and some research material he was to deliver to the British Admiralty War Office.

Just what that heavy water and material contained, we can only speculate, but it is clear that his commitment to defeating the Nazis was not the stuff of armchair declarations. Feldenkrais was a man of action, if anything, and his passion to help humankind was great. So great, in fact, that when he was asked to participate in the Manhattan Project—the secret project to build an atomic bomb—he declined. Although doing so could have made him a renowned scientist, whether by principle or fate, Feldenkrais was destined for another path altogether.

—

Shortly after fleeing to Great Britain and while stationed on a submarine as part of a research expedition, he fell and injured one of his knees which was very painful. He had previously injured the other knee playing soccer when he was 19. That first knee injury was so severe, the doctors wanted to perform surgery, and possibly amputate his leg; the options were few in those days. He refused the surgery. His decision paralleled my refusal of surgery but was much more dramatic and daring.

While recuperating, Feldenkrais had an insight based on his need to walk to the bathroom with two damaged knees. Since he had been resting so much, his brain had reorganized his system enough so he could use the originally injured leg as a support. He observed this with keen interest. His creative mind, educated in many sciences led him to devise what came to be known as the Feldenkrais Method. Essentially he was an early pioneer of what we now call neuronal plasticity.

He eventually settled in Tel Aviv in the early 1950s and began to teach his methods to others full-time. His work continued, expanding throughout Europe and North America, and by the early 1970s, he was internationally renowned.

Sadly, Feldenkrais died in 1984 from complications related to a subdural hematoma due to at least one head injury in a car accident. It was the very week I began my training in his work. There was a tremendous sense of activity and energy after his death—people were unsure what direction his longtime students, who would become the new trainers, would take his teachings. The empty space his death left became filled with new ideas and conflicts. People were excited and wondering: what next? That's when I began my training, on the edge of possibilities and promise. And what better time to begin?

I wasn't there very long before I realized that the classes were very unusual in many respects. We were not allowed to take notes, so we had to pay attention—with our our kinesthetic sensing awareness as well as our intellect. The lectures centered around the basic principles of Feldenkrais, which are many. He taught about the relationship of a human being to a changing world as well as about one's ability to move without hesitation into another position. Trying to wrap my head around Feldenkrais's style of teaching was like trying to find a path to knowledge in an empty sky, just like Buddhist teachings.

Through endless movement sequences we would not only "learn to learn" as Feldenkrais would say, but we also improved the way we moved by eliminating unnecessary movements and thus improve efficiency, which helped us develop the famously sensitive "Feldenkrais Touch."

Our brains, I learned, contain billions of neural pathways that form as we become habituated to certain patterns of thinking, acting or moving. Our neural pathways actually weave together these thoughts and actions because of our continuous, unconscious repetitions. Once these networks are formed, we move and think in familiar ways over and over again.

By introducing new opportunities, our brains actually begin to form new neural networks. What can be applied to movements, can also be applied to our thoughts—we can actually teach our bodies to generate new cellular and neural pathways and utilize tissues and muscles to regain movement that isn't associated to pain or inefficiency. And the more efficient our movements, the more energy we have to direct elsewhere. I realized as I read Feldenkrais's books and listened to the taped lectures, that the neuromuscular patterns and rigidity of our systems are learned behaviors.

We started by lying down on a thin mat on a wooden floor for hours at a time. The lesson began with a body scan, where we were told to concentrate on the sensation of our bodies contacting the floor. Whether it was the size of the space between our lower backs and the floor, or between the back of the neck and the floor, we became aware not just of the pressure of the floor on our bodies, but the emptiness that defined our structure.

ATM Lesson

The Feldenkrais Method teaches orientation in space and how people see themselves in, and move through, the world. And so it was that we started with our eyes, one of the first infant movements. During lessons, we slid our eyes to the right and to the left, making circles and arcs, and moving them up and down. We would focus on a single eye for an hour, maybe even longer, and then another day, do something similar with the other. We paid attention to our breathing as we moved, feeling our ribs rise and fall, our necks and spines sway with every breath. We focused on other parts of ourselves that moved along with our eyes. If I moved my eyes one way, I discovered, my spinal column, ribs, and clavicles followed, twisting and turning toward the path of my vision. Differentiating my eyes and immobilizing these other body parts was challenging, and as I did so, I noticed subtle tensions in my nerves and tissues.

As my eyes moved, I considered, what is exactly happening? The line in which one eye moves has a wiggle to it, does the other? Is my jaw tightening? Why? How exactly? I became increasingly aware of how the tension and anxiety I'd been experiencing was inscribed on my facial muscles, causing the features of my face to tighten even when at rest.

By differentiating the movement of a single eye and then adding the movement of the head, I discovered how connected the muscles of the eyes are to the muscles of the neck. I learned that stroke victims, or people with neck pain, for instance, often are immobilized because their eyes stare straight ahead, a fixed stare, that contributes to their inability to move. By working with just the eyes, people with such injuries can actually learn to move their neck more freely. Similarly, Moshé Feldenkrais did this with his tongue when he had a stroke not long before he died. He began by moving only his tongue, because he couldn't speak. By taking his tongue through its possible range of motion, he recovered his ability to speak.

And so it was that we lay there as if paralyzed, playing with eye movements for a long time. When we stood up, the whole class was amazed—each of us realized we were seeing the world very differently. Our eye orbit muscles had changed, and so had the tightness in our bodies. Just by changing the way our eyes moved, we could change how we saw and moved through the world! In other words, just by changing the eyes, we changed the brain. It was a fantastic sensation!

As the training progressed, I discovered that the seemingly random movements of his "lessons" were actually developmental movement sequences that took our bodies back from birth through the stages of human development, like a baby moving from her tummy to a crawling position and then pulling herself up to standing and then walking. Each small repetition refines the brain and forms new neural pathways, connecting the mind to the body, and hence changes the whole self.

The sequences we were learning were familiar, but unfortunately, having adult minds, we were far harder to teach than infants. Each of us in the class had entire lifetimes of movement and thought patterns that we were identified with. We were refining patterns into more elegant ways of moving. Each small movement was broken down into even smaller, almost microscopic movements. We really didn't know what we were doing or why we were doing it and they didn't want us to know the outcome so each exploratory movement would be fresh. For me that was one of the most exciting parts of the training: investigating and discovering the small details.

———

The lessons were rapidly changing my body image, as well as my sense of self and place in the world. I began to move with less pain as my movements became more efficient. As with any change, a big part of me resisted and I found it very scary. I was thrilled inside the classroom where I was discovering so many new ways to orient my body and conceptualize my place in the physical world, but outside the classroom, it felt as if my life was falling apart. The instantaneous relief I felt when I returned to San Francisco was swept away by powerful feelings of sadness. I found myself going home at night and weeping uncontrollably.

It was a very emotional time, and at first I attributed it to all the changes in my life. I had just left my career and my home and I was embarking on an entirely new and exciting path—but new paths can be frightening, and my insecurities began to overwhelm me. Would I be able to handle this? Did I really have what it took to make it? What kind of a practitioner would I turn out to be? These thoughts gnawed at me almost constantly, and I was very upset, crying daily. But what I didn't realize for a long time, not until I had worked with many clients and seen them go through similar stages, was that by retraining my body, I began to access emotional states from my early development—as if I were once again an infant.

Back then all I understood was everything in my life was changing and I just couldn't stop crying. I thought I was falling apart, when really, I was coming together for the first time in my life. But no one tells an infant their life has just begun, and no one was telling me that either. My body and spirit were in the process of being re-born, and just like the first time I was born into this world, it was terrifying. The only thing to do was wail, and so wail I did.

Whirlpools in the River of Life

We don't need our frontal lobes
to feel our bodies.

BONNIE BAINBRIDGE COHEN

CHANGING THE BRAIN through movement was having the same results as changing the brain through stillness. The state of a relaxed mind from the Feldenkrais Method was very much like meditation, and reminded me of a profound experience I'd once had at a retreat in Oregon with the Zen Buddhist teacher, Charlotte Joko Beck. It was a three day retreat in silent meditation and I had never before been silent for even as much as a day, much less three days. At the retreat, we dressed in dark clothing as if we were shadows, and faced the wall to meditate. We couldn't talk to anyone, except for once a day when we were permitted to speak to Joko who was guiding us. It was incredibly difficult, and by the end of the retreat I was sobbing, just as I did when I began the Feldenkrais training; the experiences triggered very deep emotions.

As I was leaving this Zen retreat, I found myself standing at my car, my brain was scrambled. I could not for the life of me figure out how to open up the car door, much less drive the car, and the sensation of not having access to my own mind was staggering. It was just like a time in the Feldenkrais Training when after a lesson I couldn't remember how to walk; and when I did my awareness was so acute that I observed a slight swagger that was causing me hip and back pain. The entire meditation experience of three days with no contact with anyone and no stimulation –just really focusing on only the breath and inner world created by the "mind talk"—was overwhelming.

I discovered that my continuing studies in Buddhism, which eventually evolved to Vajrayana or Tibetan style, helped me to focus and understand that although the way is not always clear, presence is important. For me, Buddhist practices fit perfectly with somatic or body work. Through meditation I learned to focus my awareness on breath, body and sound. By focusing on the moment, not allowing myself to dwell on the past or worry about the future but simply be in the very moment of time I was experiencing, I became more aware of the space that surrounded me—and that awareness, in turn, helped me to feel my breath, feel my body move through space with every inhalation, every exhalation, however subtly or imperceptibly. The rising and lowering of my rib cage, the gentle rocking motion of my head as I took air into my nose and let it out through my mouth, and the stretching and shrinking of my spine brought me an acute awareness that the slightest motion of my body had a powerful effect. I grew calm.

The state of non-action, of just being, enabled me to become acutely aware of how the smallest movement could lead to the greatest change, and having experienced these sensations through Buddhism, I was very prepared to trust that however frustrating the Feldenkrais training was at times, by yielding to the frustration and allowing my own energies to be redirected, I became more aware of many things. The sensation of my bare foot on a path. A tightness in one shoulder. A painful part of my sacrum. Curious, I investigated the sensations of pain.

I knew awareness was not something that would happen overnight;

developing awareness is a journey that begins before birth, and follows us through life and beyond. Sensing my bones and body on the increasingly comfortable wooden floor became grounding, a delightful respite from the emotional turmoil, and would serve to ground me in the future.

My training in Buddhism similarly helped me to see how inextricably I was linked to the earth as I became more aware of the beauty of the smallest details in nature: the curve of a leaf as it drifts slowly to the ground, the undulating shades of grays and blues and browns in a small trickling stream, the jagged edges of a cliff pressed against a soft and yielding sky. During this period, I went to Hawaii on a Zen Buddhist retreat training for six weeks, two of which were intensive. We meditated from 5 a.m. to 9 p.m. daily, with no eye contact with anyone, and no speaking to anyone except to Robert Aitken, the teacher. My brain calmed and settled from overstimulation, I discovered that sounds and colors became more vibrant, and the noise and anxious thoughts in my head subsided. I sensed how I, too, was a part of the earth's beauty, and my movements through the universe were as much a function of the universe similar to the slow, geologic transformation of the earth's crust or the rapid molecular transformation of an atomic particle.

—

When I began my graduate studies in Somatic Psychology, I learned that my advisor would be the founder of the program, Don Hanlon Johnson. I couldn't have been more fortunate. Dr. Johnson was classically trained as a psychologist at Yale, but he began to question conventional approaches to psychotherapy when he became fascinated by studies in philosophy and anthropology that challenged the western mind/body duality of western allopathic medicine. Instead, Johnson moved beyond the traditional disciplinary divides of academia that separated psychology from other social sciences and humanities. After he trained with Ida Rolf and began working as a Rolfer, he began to view healing as a holistic integration of the mind, body and spirit that draws on a multiplicity of approaches, and is connected to communities and social change.

I liked Dr. Johnson, or Don as he preferred to be called, immediately. He was a slim, handsome man with light curly hair and beard and gentle demeanor. He moved like a dancer, with an energy that appeared to have no limits. His lively, penetrating eyes revealed a rare blend of curiosity, intelligence and kindness, and I could not have asked for a better mentor.

The previous year, when I was seeking a program of graduate study, I had found that whenever I discussed my interest in the Feldenkrais Method with faculty, the response was inevitably the same. "Huh?" they would say, and "Feldenchrist? What's that?" No one appeared to have the slightest familiarity with the work.

But as soon as I met Don, his eyes lit up and his whole body became alert. "Oh? Feldenkrais?" he asked curiously, and I immediately saw he was interested. "Do you know Miriam Pfieffer?" he asked me, "I studied with her in France."

I couldn't believe he had studied with Miriam Pfieffer! From the books I had read and my talks with my trainer, I already knew that she was an important figure in the Feldenkrais community, and had been an early student of Moshé Feldenkrais. It turned out that Don used one of Feldenkrais's books in his Somatics curriculum. He was the first academic I spoke with in San Francisco who was experientially familiar with the Feldenkrais Method, and his knowledge was extensive. I couldn't have found a more perfect place to study body-based or somatic psychotherapy. I wanted to learn everything I could from him so that I could integrate psychotherapy with my future practice.

Working with him, was very exciting—clearly we were studying cutting-edge work. He was very influenced by Charlotte Selver's work "Sensory Awareness." Charlotte Selver was connected to the local Zen Buddhist group in San Francisco where she developed her work that

42

married meditation and sensing in a gentle way, connecting the body to the earth, plants and nature. Don Johnson opened many doors for me as I went through the Somatic Psychology program, and began to introduce me to other key figures, such as Gerda Alexander, the founder of "Eutony" (a method of bone and muscle tone awareness and movement) and Emilie Conrad, the founder of "Continuum Movement" (an integration of breath, sound, non-linear movement exploration and awareness). These practitioners and theorists were virtual rock stars in the field of Somatics and to be studying with them was an amazing opportunity.

—

I met Emilie Conrad when Don Johnson invited her to give a talk at our Somatics class. The minute she walked into the room, I could feel her energy. She was very mysterious and exotic looking—like a bewitching Goddess with long dark hair and a body that moved like the ocean's waves, sinuous and enticing. She had been a trance-dancer in Haiti as she developed her work, and it showed in her every motion. She enchanted us with her talk about cells and fluids and wave motion and interplanetary life and I knew right away that I wanted to study with her—which to this day, I periodically continue to do.

Her work centers on fluidity of the nervous system through non-linear, non-repetitive movements. Our movement explorations in her workshops often include building layers of resonance (prolonged, intensified vibrational wave patterns) using the breath, sound and cellular based body movements.

Emilie grew up in Brooklyn, New York in the 1930's. She nearly died at birth and had respiratory problems most of her young life, and a painful scar from an appendectomy. The child of Jewish immigrants, she felt estranged from the community around her, finding life in Brooklyn dull, dark and bleak. She began to mix with Italian and Caribbean immigrants and soon felt herself come alive as she moved into a world of dance. As a young woman she moved to Haiti and immersed herself in dance and voodoo ceremonies.

An exotic beauty, she moved back to New York, where she began modeling, a career that eventually took her to Los Angeles where she found great success. But modeling wasn't her life's dream; all the while she worked in front of the camera, she was developing her theories of life, water, fluids and wave motion, incorporating these concepts into movement work. As her theories developed, she was drawn to working with paralyzed people because she knew she had an innate gift as a healer. This work led to her theory that paralysis is a hypnotic state and can therefore be changed.

By the time she was forty, Emilie had met Dr. Valerie Hunt, who worked at UCLA in the Department of Kinesiology. Dr. Hunt was doing experiments with dancers and altered states of consciousness. She was also researching mental illness, healing and fields of resonance. Emilie became one of her research subjects. She was influenced by Dr. Hunt's work as she developed her own work that she named "Continuum." With its emphasis on nonlinear fluid movements, this work has since been used to teach both disabled and able-bodied people to find comfort in their tissues and find an alternative universe of movement by creating new tissue and neurological pathways of movement, like a serpent or water creature learning to move on land.

In her workshops we would lie on our blankets on the floor and move and tone and breathe as she suggested, having demonstrated to us possible nonlinear movements that were remarkably like a serpent. These serpentine movements and the development of resonance in the room would help us create a wave-like motion in our own bodies. By delving into our inner cellular spaces and layering in tones and unusual breathing sequences, sounds erupted sporadically from the room as we plumbed the depths of our consciousness looking for mitochondria or primal streaks to build fluidity, spaciousness, creativity and peace.

Emilie Conrad wrote a memoir of her rich life, called, *Life on Land,* and in it is a chapter on serpentology. As I read this chapter I became transfixed by her words and teachings. I began to use her workshops to reinvigorate myself according to the mysterious activities during the four-day sequences, in which there were no linear patterns of movement. Alien creatures emerged from the students and we lost our personalities and habits. It is wild work! Using Emilie's ideas, I now show some of my clients a breath to do that helps rehydrate their tissues as I work with them.

—

In addition to working with Emilie Conrad, I had an amazing opportunity to study for a weekend with Gerda Alexander, one of the European pioneers of somatic awareness work and movement. Gerda Alexander was born in 1908 in Wuppertal, Germany where she studied modern dance with Jacques Dalcroze whose ideas were known as Eurythmic Education, a kind of education based on music and dance. Dalcroze was particularly interested in the physiological explanation of musical influences, and began to work with disturbed and handicapped children and adults using movement and dance.

Gerda Alexander built on his ideas as she continued to develop her own work. She left Germany in 1929 and moved to Denmark, where she became very ill and had to give up dancing, which she so dearly loved. As the Nazis rose to power, she knew she could not return to her home country, so after her recovery she remained in Denmark, where she developed her theory of movement called Eutony, which means harmonious tonus, or tone of the body tissues. Eutony work develops a presence consisting of awareness of mind, sensation of the form of the body, and contact with one's environment, including awareness of breath, circulation, tissues, inner space and organs.

The connections between the work of Emilie Conrad and Moshé Feldenkrais and Buddhist philosophy are also apparent in Gerda Alexander's work. Even before I knew of Gerda's work I had a fascination with touching people's bones and helping them sense their skeletons, but her work gave me even more tools to transmit this awareness to my clients. By adopting some of each pioneer's work, I began to create my personal way of working.

I was absolutely thrilled when Don Johnson brought her to the program to teach a seminar on Eutony. I felt very honored to meet her because she must have been in her eighties by then, and I knew such a chance might never come again.

That weekend she took us through a variety of experiences in order to understand her work, which avoids active breathing exercises and works through indirect action on the Autonomic Nervous System. I found Eutony to be less scientific, more feminine and more intimate in its approach than the Feldenkrais Method. I later found out that Feldenkrais had studied with her! Gerda had us tap on our bones with a piece of bamboo to develop what I call "bony awareness," because of the resonance between the cellular structure of bone and bamboo. We dry-brushed our skin to better sense our boundaries and to release superficial lymph and we rested on hard chestnuts to release tight fascia. It was all very new but learning through sensation became a path to intuitive understanding. With open-ended questions, such as "What do you notice?" rather than passively recording information through the intellect alone is a very different way to absorb new experiences. We learned to feel our bodies through art and movement studies, like creating a movement sequence starting from a knee. I felt my body racing toward discovery, as if new limbs and organs were growing with every breath I took.

This experience of self-discovery would return years later after Gerda Alexander had returned to Europe and I was studying with her student,

Eutony practitioner Joyce Riveros, who is still teaching today. Joyce was teaching a ten day intensive seminar, and she included in our classes a deep study of anatomy, usually with classical music softly playing. One day, after a really long and intense day of working with our minds and stillness and tapping on our bones and brushing our skin, I began to feel an increasingly painful layer of fascia burning under me as I rested on my back. I was confused at first, but then I realized it was the beginning of an unusual release, starting at my sacrum and working up my spine, and triggering a powerful childhood memory.

When I was nine years old I fell hard on my sacrum, but rather than take me to a doctor, my parents just put tape on my back. Now, decades later, the fiery sensations I was re-experiencing caused me to weep silently from the pain and the memory of the injury. Eventually the release of fascia stopped, and I was shocked that something like that could occur in my body while doing such subtle awareness work. The experience gave me a whole new understanding of the body's ability to release a memory held in the tissue, and helped me to realize how profound a heightened body awareness can be in helping people to uncover long-buried traumas and injuries.

—

I pursued my studies in the Somatics Program. I became immersed in books and articles about the emerging professional field of Somatics and psychology, and soon I was working on my thesis and interviewing a number of women about their use of Feldenkrais Method to treat their various issues with trauma. Their stories were remarkable and demonstrated just how powerful bodywork can be in healing not just the body, but the spirit and psyche as well.

As I continued with the program, my understanding grew exponentially, each day bringing wondrous new discoveries and insights. What had once been an unfamiliar and esoteric approach to healing when I was first learning the Feldenkrais Method in Oregon, had become a powerful and affirming exploration of how one can use awareness to change patterns. One can refine the mind to become more aware by developing a profound sensory capacity through the five senses. I could even sense the difference through my touch that could now differentiate fascia, fluids and bones. Who knew that the invisible tissues deep within our flesh could have a tactile quality that we can feel? The idea was not completely new as it was being developed by others, but there was no doubting its truth as I later came to know.

My own capacity to be a practitioner, though, remained obscure. I knew I could teach, but the hands-on manual manipulation work eluded me. I didn't think of myself at all as a practitioner of the healing arts, I only I wanted to feel better. It would be some time before I was fully aware—and accepting—of my unique skill to help others. My role at this point was as a student, and as a student, it was fraught with doubts, insecurities, confusion and anxiety. I was thrilled to be learning all that I was learning and meeting such amazing people, and for the first time in my life I didn't feel alone—I belonged.

But did I really have what it took? Was I really ready to take on the immense responsibility of having someone else's traumatized body in my hands? I was simultaneously enthralled and terrified as my skills and awareness developed. As I entered my second summer in the Feldenkrais program, I found myself better prepared because I realized how little I really did know. I was learning to learn at a rapid pace.

Fear of Falling

You can, at any time of your life, rewire
yourself as long as I can convince you
that there is nothing permanent in your
system except what you believe to be so.

MOSHE FELDENKRAIS

AS MY TRAINING progressed, I became more fully aware of not only my present state, but my primordial state. That is, my awareness of my body and senses took me further and further back to where it all began, which was with the formation of my flesh inside my mother's womb. Some say that humans are unable to remember their births, but I have discovered that when the mind's neural pathways, have been changed, it is surprising what can be remembered.

I was not unfamiliar with the concept of birth memories. Years before, when I was living in Oregon, Rebirthing Therapy was all the rage and there was a very popular book on the topic that everyone I knew was talking about, called *Rebirthing in the New Age* by Leonard Orr. I thought the whole thing was totally weird, but it fascinated me nonetheless, so I got the book and began reading. The idea that we cannot remember our births, I learned, is based on the idea that our brains at birth have not yet formed the capacity to store memories, particularly long-term ones. Orr explained that there exists a form of memory at the cellular level.

This cellular memory is distributed throughout the body's tissues, organs, bones, and fluids and leads us to intuitively react to external stimuli based upon ideas we formed at birth. In other words, because all birth is traumatic, when we are born we are terrified and form certain assumptions about the world, which we then repeat throughout life. People born through forceps delivery, as I was, for example, might rely on others to pull them out of a difficult situation and become terrified when they are left on their own. Or, as in my case, they may desperately resist leaving places of security, such as homes.

Reading these ideas really impressed me because it was as if all the anxiety and fears of my life finally began to make sense. How could I not have been terrified at birth, and how could those forceps have done anything but traumatize me even further? What could I possibly have done with that trauma but retain it in some way, buried deeply in the molecular matrix of my flesh and fluids, pain residing in the curve of my spine, or the rapid beat of my terrified heart? Although my brain may not have remembered it, my cells had, and my brain in turn reacted with my cells to lead me into a pattern of constantly re-enacting the fear and pain I felt as I was pulled so forcefully and violently from my mother's warm and comforting womb into the harsh and glaring lights and sounds of the world.

Reading *Rebirthing in the New Age* helped me to become more open to the possibility that my conscious mind was only one level of awareness. But I wanted to learn more, particularly about the breathing techniques the book discussed. I was already focusing on my breath in meditation and yoga. Orr wrote that by learning to connect to our breath, we can facilitate our healing and alleviate anxiety. From my experience with meditation, it made sense to me, but he took it far beyond relaxation to show how the body can reach a primordial pre-conscious state that actually returns the body to a state of fetal relaxation. I was intrigued.

There was a phone number in the back of the book, so I called it. A woman named Norma answered the phone and said that the person listed on the book was no longer there, but that she was a Rebirthing therapist and could help me. Despite rethinking my own birth trauma, I really wasn't all that interested in their claim that people could recall birth memories, at that point; I understood the basic concept, but what I was really intrigued by was the concept of breathwork. So I said as much, and explained that I wanted to learn more.

Norma agreed to work with me and shortly after, we met. She was a very petite, small-boned woman with short brown hair that gave her an almost nun-like appearance. She had just returned from India, and the trip seemed to have left her with an almost ethereal sense of calm that somehow fit perfectly with her vibrant and dynamic energy. The duality of these two seemingly diverse traits gave her a warm and maternal nature that immediately put me at ease.

I began to work one-on-one with Norma. The idea was to relax into that primordial state of the womb until we reached a state between consciousness and pre-consciousness, replicating our gestational awareness.

But it wasn't easy to endure. At first I would reach a point of discomfort and restlessness and wanted to get up.

"You've reached the point of resistance," Norma calmly explained, softly pressing my shoulder back to the floor. "This is precisely the time to go deeper."

Her gentle smile was reassuring. I knew that by breaking through resistance, I would reach a point where I could experience breakthroughs in my awareness. These breakthroughs would enable me to retrieve my cellular memories and incorporate them into my consciousness. So trusting Norma, I relaxed and forced myself to lay longer, breathing rhythmically until I found myself drifting off to sleep.

"This is embarrassing!" I told her when I caught myself in mid-snore and realized I'd fallen asleep. "I'm trying to relax but I keep drifting off to sleep!"

"That's because it's working," she said, "your body is recalling the anesthesia your mother received during your birth, and you are re-enacting your drugged state."

Well, maybe, I thought.

I also began to experience a sense of falling when I relaxed, something I'd experienced often since a child, usually during a twilight state of sleep or just as I was drifting off to sleep. I wasn't sure what to make of that, but it would jolt me out of a relaxed state, leaving me frustrated and perplexed.

Norma was trained in several different therapeutic models, and I found that working with her helped to anchor me as I was going through so much change in my life. Rebirthing Therapy rekindled an interest in my birth and I asked my mother about it. When she described the way she was knocked out by drugs and the whole forceps delivery and how I was taken to a separate room and left untouched and put on a feeding schedule, then sent home to be bottle fed, I was just amazed. I'd heard bits and pieces of the story before, but now that I was a woman myself and had a better sense of what having a baby entailed, I was appalled at the cold, clinical approach to something so natural and intimate as giving birth to a baby.

"Mom? How could you let them do that?" I asked her.

"I know, Judith, but that's just the way they did it back then," she said, uncomfortable with the topic of conversation. "It was the modern way. We just didn't know any better back then. After the war, everything about medicine and science was so new that we just trusted the doctors knew what they were doing. Besides, you haven't turned out so bad, just look at all you've accomplished."

I knew she was proud of me, but I felt like my whole life had been one big snarl of anxiety, and I wanted it to be released!

"Well there's something that I still don't understand," I said, still hungering for answers. "Ever since I was a little girl I have had this sudden sensation of falling. Did I ever fall when I was a baby?"

"No, of course not! I would never let my babies fall!" My mother retorted. But I could tell the question made her uncomfortable, so over time, I would return to it, until one day she finally confessed that it was true.

I could tell that memory really upset my mother, and I didn't press it any further. I didn't need to, I was just pleased to finally have an explanation for why I kept having that sensation of falling. Shortly after that experience, I found in Feldenkrais' book *The Elusive Obvious*(1981) some very interesting information about the body's anxiety pattern, the eighth and tenth cranial nerves and the olive (part of the brainstem, inside the neck):

> ...at the superior olive, strong incitations, produced
> by very loud noises, will diffuse and excite the tenth
> cranial nerve, instrumental in holding the breath...
> the vestibular branch of the eighth cranial nerve
> innervates (the inner ear) and the reaction that
> the adult interprets as fear of falling is inherited,
> inborn and needs no personal experience before it is
> operative...the first experience of anxiety is therefore
> connected with a stimulation of the vestibular
> branch of the eighth cranial nerve. (p.58-59)

My body was remembering. It was remembering sensation and I had to be careful how I interpreted the memory. Little did I realize that I would remember much more about my birth, such as how descending down the birth canal actually felt and the terror of the feel of the forceps, when I began to work with Dr. John Upledger a few years later.

As my M.A. studies progressed, I left the Rebirthing work behind as I experimented more and more with many new forms of therapy. We had dance and art therapy classes and studied psychopathology and cross-cultural psychology and cross-cultural healing, as well as Encounter Therapy groups and Transpersonal Psychology. There was very little traditional psychology, except for psychopathology and sex therapy. I was immersed in the somatic experiences of psychology and learning about somatic history and its early beginnings in Europe, which just enthralled me. We studied the work of the psychologists Wilhelm Reich and Robert Assagioli and Carl Jung; I was especially intrigued by Jung's work with dreams, and devoured books and articles on Jungian psychology.

We also studied many women in the field. I was really surprised at how many fascinating, well-educated European women were involved in the development of Somatics or bodywork, such as Marion Rosen, Gerda Alexander, Ilse Middendorf and others. A lot of women from Europe were developing all kinds of healing techniques that utilized sensory awareness and breathwork. They were very often the wives of prominent therapists, and perhaps they formed their own women's groups to address the concerns of women. Learning about these women and the philosophies and healing techniques they'd developed was fascinating, and I knew then that I was on the right course—to become a healing practitioner in their tradition of healing through body and breathwork.

Perseverance Furthers

The soul of man, with all the streams
of pure living water, seems to dwell
in the fascia of his body.

ALEXANDER TAYLOR STILL, 1899

THE FIRST TWO years of graduate school were rigorous, but I discovered that the hard work was just beginning. One of the methods that we learned in the Feldenkrais Training was called Functional Integration. Functional Integration (FI) is the "hands on" aspect of the Feldenkrais Method. In FI, the practitioner creates the conditions using touch where the student learns to recognize what they do and explore new options to change and improve themselves. The student remains in a relaxed position, either lying, sitting or standing, while the practitioner moves them in precise ways. During a lesson, the practitioner may touch the feet, toes and ankles, gently moving them into various positions to teach the person other ways to function and to give the person a sense of how their whole self is connected.

In 1984, many of the students in my Feldenkrais Training had some sort of experience in physical therapy or physiology. It seemed as if everyone had been professionally trained in one or another aspect of the human body before they came to the program, and I felt so frustrated to be such a novice. It turned out that my teachers were thrilled that I *didn't* have that training—there was that much less for me to have to relearn, it turned out.

Still, it wasn't easy. When we moved to Functional Integration, I felt even more overwhelmed—this was the stage where I began to experience the transition from student to practitioner. I was a novice, and I had many years of training ahead of me before I could competently practice the method myself, but the reality of accepting that soon I would be laying my hands on other people was a very frightening—and exhilarating—feeling, and the confidence of my teachers gave me the courage I needed.

I discuss FI with Miriam Pfeiffer

The work we experienced was so gentle that during some of the first FI lessons, my sense was that the practitioner was hardly doing anything, especially compared to the chiropractic work I'd previously experienced. Yet even though I could barely sense the practitioner's suggestions through their gentle touch, it seemed that no matter what "problem" I presented, when each lesson was finished my entire body would feel radically altered. My vision was crystal sharp, colors appeared brighter, my feet felt as if they were fully contacting the floor, I was more balanced, was more erect and centered; and I even felt taller and lighter as I moved. It was an amazing sensation, and completely bewildering considering how subtle each guiding hand's touch had been.

But what was most surprising was not how radically altered my body became, but how radically altered I became as I continued the lessons. Because the work involved changing the nervous system, I discovered that all kinds of social, behavioral and emotional patterns began to change. Just as I had found myself sobbing continuously when I first started the program, as time went on I began having the most vivid dreams and I had an amazingly strong ability to recall the details of my dreams. My artistic nature blossomed, and most importantly, people began to comment on how insightful and aware I was becoming. I had always been the type of person who wanted to help others—that was why I went into teaching in the first place and into bodywork subsequently—but the further I went into the programs the more people began commenting on what a gifted therapist or practitioner I was becoming.

"Me? Gifted?" I would laugh, as if the idea were preposterous. But most therapists, I later learned, don't necessarily realize their gifts until they are well developed. The gift of healing is curious—it is not something one seeks out, not even something one can develop consciously beyond a certain level. One learns to get out of the way of a process. The ability to touch another person with awareness and have information transmitted from the practitioner to the client in a way that goes directly to the source of a person's suffering: that ability is a gift.

—

When the Feldenkrais training ended, I had to make some decisions. My coursework was over in the Somatics Program and it was time to get started on my thesis; but over the course of the year, I had met a man and fallen in love—and he wanted to leave San Francisco and move to Seattle. I was torn—I loved San Francisco, but I also wanted a stable relationship and had already been through enough failed relationships that I wasn't going to let another one fail without giving it every chance to become lasting. I met with Don Johnson and he assured me that I could work on my thesis in Seattle and mail my chapters back to him as I went along—this was before email and the internet, so everything was typed on a typewriter, photocopied and sent by U.S. mail. It would be a lot of work, but it seemed like a workable solution, so that was what I did.

I could tell even before I left that I was going to have a hard time with my thesis. First, I'd never written anything like that before—an entire thesis, which is practically a book! The thought of it was just immense, but I knew if I focused and worked one chapter at a time, I would finish it.

Would my professor and mentor be pleased? Now that was the real hurdle. For as much as my professor was excited about my Feldenkrais work, he remained an academic, and whenever we discussed my thesis, we seemed to clash.

"You're approaching this with too much of a bias," he would say, and my heart would fall and my mind race. How could he say that? I wondered, he had been encouraging me every step of the way and now that it was time to actually start doing my research, he was telling me I was doing it all wrong?

"But not many people have ever looked at bodywork in this way before," I would say, defending my position, "I'm going to show how it's so much more effective than talk therapy."

"That's the problem," he would counter, "You've already made up your mind what you are going to find. You are letting your bias for bodywork influence your findings before you've even begun your research."

I just couldn't understand how he could be so sold on bodywork and then turn around and tell me that I shouldn't be sold on it myself; he was completely perplexing and sometimes impossible to please—I completely understood everything he was saying in class and in his writings, so why couldn't I understand him now? Or more accurately, why couldn't he understand what I was trying to do? It slowly dawned on me that he was teaching me to become observant and impartial. Ultimately I realized that regardless of how I felt, I'd have to bring in other perspectives and let the readers make the final decision themselves.

I finally understood what everyone was trying to teach me—that there is no one way and the path has no beginning and no end. And so it would be with all my education.

—

When I arrived in Seattle, I rented a small house near my boyfriend where I set up my Feldenkrais practice. Even though I was still in training, I was eager to get started and I knew enough to begin working with clients as I continued returning to San Francisco in the summers to complete the Feldenkrais program. So one of the first things I did contact other Feldenkrais practitioners. I was really surprised to discover that unlike San Francisco, where there were many alternative movement therapists, there were only five or six people in all of Seattle who practiced the Feldenkrais Method. Of course, in San Francisco I was surrounded by Somatics classmates and teachers of the Feldenkrais Method, but still, I was surprised to realize that such a powerful technique remained relatively obscure in a progressive city like Seattle. But that turned out to be a good thing for me, because it enabled me to launch my practice while I completed my training and thesis. And with so few practitioners, I had little competition—and a great deal of interest, it turned out.

I discovered that the whole business end of starting a practice was a bit overwhelming, but it fell into place so easily that I didn't really have time to worry about it. I began meeting with the other Feldenkrais practitioners and soon one of them, Jeff Haller, really helped me to have the confidence—and the know-how—to get started. Jeff was an intense, energetic man; at six and a half feet tall with iridescent blue eyes, he was hard to miss. Jeff had played to basketball in college, but after discovering Feldenkrais, he left sports to train to be a Feldenkrais Practitioner. He was as amazing to watch as he was to listen to—he was a head taller than anyone in the group, with long arms and legs that moved with such grace he appeared more like a lithe dancer than a basketball player. And as a practitioner, he was equally amazing; he had an incredibly tender and precise touch, and his sensitivity was unmatched. Everyone was drawn to Jeff's magnetic energy, and he quickly became a leader in establishing the Feldenkrais Method in Seattle and eventually became an international trainer for the Method. He was clearly driven and ambitious, and his enthusiasm was contagious. Everyone around Jeff was inspired to work harder, do better, and give more, and I was no exception.

"Just remember, Judith," he said to me, "You don't have to do anything but put your full awareness into your touch when you work with someone and that will help them to change their ability to be present. If they come to you because their knee is hurting, just touch their knee and be totally present with them and you'll discover a presence inside of you that you never even realized you had. And you'll also change their awareness of their knee pain, and how they use their knee."

Jeff understood my involvement in buddhist meditation and his guidance really helped me to see that I could make a difference, and that no matter what obstacles I encountered, I would be successful. But first, I had to figure out how to get clients.

I set up a room in my house where I would work with clients, and had a friend build me a table where they would lie for the "lessons," as they are called. It was a very calming room with soft, earthy colors, and some beautiful Buddhist prints and carvings. And then I just began putting small posters all over the city—in coffee houses, book stores, natural food stores—and pretty soon, people started to know my name just from the posters they saw everywhere.

When Jeff set up a Seattle Feldenkrais Professional Training Program (1988), I decided to set up my new out-of-home office in the same space. I wanted to be immersed in the work and I hoped people would meet me when I observed the training classes and then start coming to me for private lessons. Students were curious about my experiences in my own earlier training program and wanted to experience my sense of touch.

I also set up a table at the Fremont Fair—an annual event in the artistic area of Seattle—and I would give five minute lessons to anyone who wanted one. They would discover these little lessons were so powerful that they began coming to my classes at our Feldenkrais Center, and from there, to my private sessions. It all happened so synergistically that my practice just took off right from the start—a sign from the universe that I was exactly where I was supposed to be in my life and in this world. And I just loved interacting and teaching people what I was learning.

I began working on my M.A. thesis and began sending my chapters back to Don Johnson and he'd make his critiques and send them back to me and I'd make the revisions he requested and send them back. My thesis writing progressed over the next nine months, going back and forth until we were both pleased with its development and I came closer and closer to my master's degree, until at last, Don told me he was happy with my thesis and my graduate work was complete. It had been a tremendous amount of work, but I had persevered and was gaining a tremendous amount of knowledge in return.

For all the frustration and hard work, however, it was certainly worth it. The more I got into the Feldenkrais work, the more I discovered that my training in Somatic Psychotherapy had given me a unique perspective and ability that I felt was missing in the Feldenkrais community in 1984. Many of the practitioners seemed astute, but they were not always comfortable with the emotions of their clients. That was unfortunate, I felt, because one of the things that happens when a person goes through a life change is that some emotions are released as the central nervous system tissues change. My training in the Somatic Psychotherapy program, along with my own rich emotional world, prepared me well for these clients. I wasn't the least bit afraid of dealing with emotions—if a client wanted to cry, I let them cry, and witnessed those intense emotions with them.

As a result of my willingness to work with emotions, many of my colleagues began sending me abuse victims—this was in the mid to late 1980's when the reality of just how great a problem sexual abuse can be, was finally coming to light, so many women began coming to me with sad and traumatic histories of abuse. Sometimes this abuse was uncovered in the course of a treatment itself—I might be working the ankle, for example, which would affect the pelvic area, and release somatic memories of abuse in that region. They were intense sessions, but I found that by helping such wounded women to heal from those past traumas, my gifts for being present for their healing were becoming more developed.

However, I never wanted to rely upon just one paradigm of healing in my practice. My own interests as a client and patient were always much more holistic, and I had always sought out different forms of healing, whether through dance therapy, yoga, Somatic Psychotherapy or Feldenkrais. So I continued deeper studies of other healing techniques, such as Gerda Alexander's Eutony, Milton Erickson's hypnotherapy, and Emilie Conrad's Continuum, incorporating them into my practice. But still, I felt restless; there just didn't seem to be the space for therapeutic emotional release that I was really looking for. There was something missing in my practice that I just couldn't put my finger on, and that emptiness resonated with my personal anxiety. I was doing a great job of helping my clients, but I knew I could help them more; meanwhile my own life seemed to be way beyond anything I could handle—but how could that be? My career was going well, and I was building a strong, loving support network of friends and colleagues in Seattle.

———

After I'd been in practice for a couple of years and was in my last year of training in the Feldenkrais program, Margie, one of my classmates was working with another student, and called out, "Do you want to feel this cranial rhythm? It's very cool!"

Well none of us had any idea what she was talking about, but of course we all wanted to feel it because everyone was studying all kinds of somatic things. Margie had been studying something called Cranio-Sacral Therapy, which I didn't know anything about at the time.

At any rate, one by one, we all laid our hands on the back of the neck of the student she was working with, and one by one everyone expressed wonder.

"Wow!" they would say, or "I feel it!" I could tell that whatever it was they were feeling was very powerful, so I couldn't wait until it was my turn.

At first I didn't feel anything, but Margie helped guide my hands and told me to just relax and feel the gentle pulse with my whole hand. It was a lighter sensing touch than I had been using in my Feldenkrais work. Sure enough, as soon as I did as she'd instructed, I felt a steady pulse on the back of the head, just where the spinal cord enters the cerebellum. It was amazing to feel such rhythmic subtlety.

"That's called 'the cranial rhythm'," Margie explained, and told us how this doctor, John Upledger, had discovered it while working as an osteopathic physician.

A mysterious rhythm deep inside the body. What a curious concept. I couldn't wait to learn more, and from that moment on, I was hooked. I had to find this man John Upledger and learn everything I could about CranioSacral Therapy.

And then my life began to really change.

Dr. John and the Snake

Trust the process, help the people,
subordinate your ego and stay out of jail.

JOHN UPLEDGER

JOHN UPLEDGER WAS an osteopathic physician and Professor of Bio-mechanics at Michigan State University in the late 1970's and early 1980's when he found himself assisting a neurosurgeon and accidently stumbled upon a profound discovery. He was using two pairs of surgical forceps to grasp the dura—the membrane surrounding the brain and spinal cord—of a patient while the surgeon scraped away a calcified patch of tissue. But no matter how carefully Dr. Upledger tried to restrain the dura, he felt it moving forward and backward in a rhythm. The surgeon cursed him for his inability to control the membrane, while Upledger tried to explain that it was moving of its own accord—something the surgical staff had never heard of before. John Upledger began to closely observe what was happening.

Although it was moving, he saw that the rhythm of the dura did not match the respiration nor the heart beat of the patient. These movements were clearly displayed on the monitors, and were very different from the movements he was seeing and feeling.

After the surgery, Upledger thought a lot about this unexplained phenomenon. He recalled that while in osteopathic medical school he had heard about, but mostly ignored, information about William Sutherland's (1873-1954) findings regarding what he called the Primary Respiration Mechanism and the precise movement of each of the bones of the cranium as they moved in time to this rhythm. At that time, Dr. Upledger wasn't interested in this but now, he was very interested in the relevance of Sutherland's discovery, a half a century earlier, to the movement of the dura he had felt and seen during surgery. Sutherland had developed a hands-on method to mobilize the individual bones and enhance the rhythm. Although he achieved great results in cases that traditional osteopathy could not help, his work was largely pushed aside and forgotten as advances in modern medicine gave greater emphasis to technology, surgery and pharmacological innovations.

Like his predecessor Alexander Taylor Still, the founder of Osteopathy (1828-1917), Sutherland understood the importance of proper alignment and functioning for the health of the body. A.T. Still challenged 19th century methods of medicine which often harmed people instead of helping them and focused on correcting the causes of disease, not just the symptoms. In 1892, A.T. Still established the American School of Osteopathy in Kirksville, Missouri (now the Andrew Taylor Still University) and it was at this university that Dr. Sutherland as well as Dr. Upledger had studied.

Dr. Upledger devoted himself to learning all he could in the field of cranial osteopathy and over the years put together a powerful collection of techniques, many of which had their origins in Dr. Sutherland's studies. Upledger called this work CranioSacral Therapy(CST) and he spent the rest of his life teaching and developing this method.

He began by leading a research team of anatomists, physiologists, biophysicists and bioengineers at Michigan State University to investigate the phenomenon of rhythmic movement in the cranium and was able to confirm that the movement was real and measurable and that the bone sutures were not fused in adulthood as was previous understood.

In his clinical work, he broke new ground by using CranioSacral Therapy in the treatment of autistic children and began to get encouraging results. Since there were hardly any osteopaths with cranial osteopathic training in Michigan, and there were many children needing treatment, he broke with convention and taught the caregivers how to do the gentle techniques of CST. He was so impressed with how well they learned the techniques that he came to understand the necessary qualifications to do this work were a loving attitude and a sensitive touch rather than medical training. He became even more of a renegade osteopath because he went on to teach both medically and non-medically trained people around the globe and further alienated himself from the traditional osteopathic community. Although many scoffed at his discoveries, and he found himself ridiculed by many of his colleagues, Dr. Upledger continued to get astounding positive results that couldn't be ignored.

He later moved to Florida where he opened a private practice and continued to teach. He also ran a clinic for drug addicts; having grown up as a gang member in Detroit, he had just the right temperament for the task.

By 1985, his work was in such demand that he could not meet all the requests to teach and so he founded two centers in West Palm Beach, Florida: the Upledger Institute International to train teachers who could disseminate the work of CranioSacral Therapy to therapists internationally, and the Upledger Clinic to treat patients for pain and various physical, emotional and spiritual challenges. The clinic grew enormously as patients with everything from headaches to cancer, spinal cord lesions and nervous system disorders were experiencing unexpected improvements. Soon, word of the phenomenal results and powerful techniques grew, and thousands of practitioners—from body workers to physicians and dentists—were attending training programs.

CranioSacral therapy not only includes techniques to mobilize the bones of the head and tailbone but also the connective tissue (fascia); and to identify and remove energetic blocks which can hinder healing. In the course of working with thousands of patients, Dr. Upledger found that his hands were often drawn into a vortex of energy emanating from the patients body. He called this an "energy cyst" as it felt like a walled off area of disorganized energy which when released could resolve longstanding pain and disability patterns—often at a distance from the cyst itself.

> The cyst is hotter, more energetic, less organized and
> less functional than the surrounding tissues. It can result
> from physical trauma, pathogenic invasion, physiological
> dysfunction, mental and/or emotional problems
> and (possibly) spiritual problems as well. Sometimes
> malfunctioning chakras are hosts to energy cysts...."
>
> *CranioSacral Therapy II: Beyond the Dura*, 1987, p.213

He also found that through deep relaxation, he could help his patients access what he termed the "Inner Physician" or inner wisdom—an intuitive, innate self-knowledge of what exactly is wrong with the body. By facilitating the patient to call on his or her own inner physician to assist him, Dr. Upledger found his patients connecting with their nonconscious minds and discovering what was causing their health problems. In other words, our bodies have an intuitive knowledge of what has caused a breakdown in the body's functions, and through trained observation and fine tuned sensitivity, a therapist can help the patient to uncover this inner wisdom and continue the healing process in a different way. This aspect of his work he eventually developed into what he named SomatoEmotional Release(SER), after the Greek word, Soma, meaning body.

By the time I heard of his work, CST and SER were in being taught all over the United States and I was able to take my first class in Seattle. I was absolutely thrilled to learn that Dr. John, as he was affectionately called, would be coming to San Francisco for seminars over the next few years. I charged my credit cards "to the max" to study at his Institute. I met Dr. John when he was in his fifties and newly experimenting with SER. His courses ranged from very detailed osteopathic manipulation skills, to off-body energetic work, brain release and immune system treatments to dissection work where the students also participated.

I also assisted him in classes and in his clinical practice; and I was fortunate to receive treatments from him. His hands were like giant energetic clams molding to my body, deeply changing body tissues and consciousness.

Once, during the night after I received a treatment from him, I dreamed that there was a snake in my ribcage, embracing my heart and wrapped around my spinal column. In that session he had helped me find my Inner Physician or Guide which I felt was an angelic presence. I wondered for a long time about the meaning of the snake.

As much as I had found the Feldenkrais Method to be an amazing key to understanding the human body, as a therapist I found it somewhat limiting because it didn't seem to accommodate human emotion very well. I had been working with clients long enough by that time to have found that many of them came to me in a heightened emotional state, and they were as much in need of healing their spirits as their bodies. I realized that Moshe's teachings would always inform my work; but I didn't realize then that I was moving into the osteopathic world as much as I could without becoming a physician. CST and SER were different in a way that really spoke to me.

—

Dr. Upledger had developed the concept of SomatoEmotional Release with biophysicist Zvi Karni, and together they helped revolutionize the field of bodywork. By accessing a person's tissue memory through light touch and attention, involuntary body movements could be triggered—sometimes so subtly that the person was often virtually unaware of any movement at all themselves—but a skilled practitioner could detect them. Energetic forces from injuries, for example, could be trapped in the body as energy cysts causing discomfort. Pain or illness are often messages from the body trying to communicate something. We learned how to help the client tap into a pattern like this and give it an opportunity to release. These movements could result in muscle and fascial release accompanied by a spontaneous release of emotion. But what was really fascinating was that when this emotional release did occur, the client could experience a total body release, with the tissues throughout the body moving into new, more relaxed and aligned positions. As clients experienced SER, they discovered that during or within twenty-four to forty-eight hours after a treatment, they would experience a flood of emotions or dreams, often linked to past traumas associated with whatever had been accessed. These traumas had been buried in the non-conscious, retaining discomfort or stress in the body and mind until finally released through CST and SER techniques.

Working with Dr. John and a patient, 1993.

My training in Upledger's approach couldn't have come at a better time. The work was relatively new when I began my studies, so skilled practitioners were in demand, and many people were interested in my work. I began building up my toolbox of skills, taking many courses at the Upledger Institute—Visceral Manipulation with Dr. Jean-Pierre Barral, Lymphatic Drainage Therapy with Dr. Bruno Chikly and Mechanical Link with Dr. Paul Chauffour. These osteopathic teachers all drew on soft tissue manual manipulative work and body energy work, which organically grew from light touch palpation, as I had learned in Feldenkrais and more deeply with John Upledger. The education pushed me to a skill level of practice that allowed me to work in a way I had never imagined was possible.

Keeping the body free of tissue and energetic restrictions, I learned, is key to unrestricted mobility, improved motility of the individual tissues, and hence, to good health. I was interested in bridging the medical model of human healthcare with Somatics and manual therapy; the Feldenkrais Method, which mostly focused on movement education, didn't seem to me to be able to help me make this bridge.

I had clients coming to me for post-surgical work, or to avoid surgery, to correct jaw and dental trauma, or treat neck and spinal injuries, stomach aches, lung and throat problems and all sorts of mysterious pains and illnesses that no conventional, allopathic physician could diagnose or shift through allopathic medicine. Yet most physicians, I discovered, had not learned the palpation skills my colleagues and I had perfected, so we were often able to do more for a patient just by releasing tissue restrictions, than an allopathic physician can do with a pharmacopeia of medicines or through surgery. For example, we learned to help stomachs or brains function more efficiently by correcting the tissue structure. And many times the answer to the ill health was uncovered in an SER session, linking body, mind and spirit to achieve full body healing. As a result of all the health problems I was seeing in my clients who had found no success through traditional medicine, the need to integrate alternative therapies with allopathic medicine seemed to me to be urgent. And I felt CST was precisely the approach to take to help me achieve that end.

As my expertise developed, I began working with other CST practitioners. One of the most powerful methods I learned was multi-hand treatment. Multi-hand treatment simply means two or more practitioners work simultaneously on a single patient. The multiple hands (and gifts) of extra healers provides a synergy to the treatment, and allows us to go deep into the process of releasing deep, full-body tensions. I used, and still use, Feldenkrais techniques at the end of a session to be sure the client experiences their whole self in their "new" world.

I had a wonderful opportunity to see for myself how amazing the process was when an acquaintance of mine who worked as a physical therapist asked if I would assist with a client who had injured himself in a skiing accident. He had been riding in a chairlift, she explained, when it broke from the cable. Seeing it was about to crash, he jumped 30 feet from the chair, landing in the soft snow. From such a height he was injured badly, with pain in his back, neck and shoulders.

Although not rare, men were much less likely to pursue bodywork as a treatment of choice, so I was pleasantly surprised when I learned how open he was to our methods. His name was Rick, and he was in his early thirties, with a whole litany of past injuries from skiing and bicycle racing. Three of us worked on him that day and he was so relieved by our treatment that he wanted to know more. I excitedly explained about my teaching work at the Feldenkrais Center. The Center was offering a course for ski instructors at the time, and when I learned that Rick was a ski instructor himself, I sent him to the classes, and before long, he was attending regular classes in Awareness Through Movement.

Everything about my career seemed to be falling into place through such serendipitous moments. I would meet someone and soon they would be interested in my work, take my classes and eventually work with me individually, and often begin taking the classes of my colleagues and being treated by them as well. And in turn, they would send me students and clients, and just like that, my practice grew organically and exponentially until I was busier than I'd ever been before.

—

Then, one day at the Feldenkrais Center, Jeff brought me a bombshell.

"Judith, I hate to tell you this," he told me one afternoon, "but I've finally decided I'm going to close the Center." He could have knocked me over with a feather, I was so surprised.

"Close the Center!?" I asked, "You can't do that! It's the only Feldenkrais Center in the entire northwest!"

"Well," he said decisively. "We have really built a beautiful place, but it's just too expensive to sustain without my being here full-time. I will be traveling a lot more because my passion and destiny is to become a trainer in the Method, so I'm going to close it when the lease expires at the end of the month."

The end of the month. Thirty days. Well that certainly left me in a quandary; what would I do? The Center was bringing me so many clients, that if it closed, my business might really slow down. But I could see Jeff's point; he had put everything into it, and he had built such a fantastic center, but he was right. It was just too large, too expensive, way beyond anything that could sustain itself.

But as always happens, when the universe takes something away, it always gives back.

———

It just so happened that a physician I had met through my social network of healers had established a holistic health clinic that combined allopathic, or western medicine, with alternative healing or complementary healthcare. Conventionally trained medical doctors worked alongside naturopathic physicians, acupuncturists, massage therapists, hypnotherapists, and other practitioners whose work had been proven to be beneficial to patients.

When I told him that the Feldenkrais Center would be closing and asked if there was room at his clinic, he told me he would love to have me practicing there. He was especially interested in CranioSacral Therapy and Visceral Manipulation.

The opportunity to work among such diverse healers was fantastic! Not only would I have access to medically challenged clients when they were referred from physicians, but I would be working alongside physicians who genuinely appreciated the benefits of alternative healing! As I've said, more than anything, I wanted to help bridge the divide between alternative and conventional medicine. Conventional allopathic medicine is life-saving, I knew, but it has its limits for deeper healing. Many medical doctors have been trained to treat body parts, not people, and by focusing on parts of the body in isolation from the whole person, total healing just doesn't happen, at least not as well as it can.

When a person is suffering and goes to see a conventional doctor, the doctor will focus on what is most easily observed and treatable, and that usually means deciding what can be cut out, burned off, or treated with drugs. The drugs that are given to a patient almost always have side-effects that create even more health problems, and a surgery may create different problems like scar tissue issues.

But more importantly, many doctors are trained to emotionally distance themselves from their patients, and that means not being sensitive to what is really going on with the patient. And that approach is emphasized by the pressure to treat as many patients as possible in a given day. Medical doctors don't have the time to spend with a patient to really find out what is going on with them, and as medicine becomes increasingly corporatized, patients are routinely shuffled from one doctor to another.

But alternative practitioners do have time for patients, and we are trained to work with the entire patient: body, mind and spirit, rather than just their kidneys or their lungs. And we work best when we work in cooperation with other caregivers, so that there is a synergistic effect of our combined approaches. What that means is that the combination of our skills is worth more than our individual contributions—our impact is magnified by working cooperatively to heal a patient through many approaches to restoring balance and health. By working with naturopathic and conventional physicians, massage therapists and homoeopaths, for example, we provide patients whole body wellness that very often leaves them even stronger and with more vitality than before their health suffered, and with more self-care skills.

Naturally, I was thrilled to set up my practice in Seattle Healing Arts, a clinic based on a model where the patients are a priority. I soon began to thrive as I was living my dream: to bridge the somatic and medical worlds. After many years, I realized that there was something intimate and convenient about seeing clients away from a clinical setting, to encourage healing in a different, less clinical environment. That perhaps the bridge to healing was between the client and nature, or perhaps within the client that a peaceful setting could foster. So I began to consider that maybe it was time to buy a home. If I bought a home I could convert a garage or other space into a studio, and eventually see clients both at work and at home, the perfect set up as far as I was concerned. And with any luck, I thought, perhaps over time I would be able to work solely in my own private space.

As if by magic, the perfect home became available—a cozy little cottage with a large garden in the north end of Seattle, with a garage that was already set up as a studio. It wasn't much of a studio and would need some remodeling, but I bought the house, and made plans to fix it up in my spare time while working at the clinic full time. A phase of my own healing came from transforming that house and garden.

At the same time, I was taking classes with Dr. Upledger and Dr. Barral, and learning so much. I was amazed at the impact it had on my practice as patients began to recover almost miraculously from chronic pain, serious injuries and even life-long debilitating suffering. Over time, my healing work was moving more exclusively toward CranioSacral Therapy and Visceral Manipulation, and I began to incorporate techniques from hypnotherapy and Jungian dream interpretation as I talked with my clients while my hands gently manipulated their cranial bones, tissues, spines and limbs.

My hands were becoming expert in sensing the most imperceptible changes in a client's body and eventually I didn't even have to touch a client to feel the "problem" that emanated from their bodies. Just as

Dr. Upledger had taught, I was beginning to feel energies inside bodies that I'd never before noticed, and sense points of resistance that were subtle but clear. Just the slightest manipulation could release a cascade of restrictions that clients very often didn't even know they had until they stood up and realized they felt more free and alive than ever before. It was an amazing and exciting experience to facilitate healing, mature and feel my hands come alive as they never had before. I couldn't have been happier.

—

And I couldn't have been more conflicted.

The anxiety had crept up on me, coming bit by bit in moments of nervousness or worry. I hadn't previously thought of myself as a nervous person, but as time went on, different things began to make me nervous and I couldn't stop thinking about them. If I were leaving my house, I'd get very nervous until I was out of the house. If I was going to the airport, I didn't worry about flying, but the thought of leaving my home filled me with anxiety. It would come over me like a veil, uncontrollable and though I never thought that something bad would actually happen, for some reason I would spin out of control whenever I had to leave my house.

I also became very concerned about not forgetting anything. If I were supposed to run an errand, pick up something at a grocery store, take care of some detail, and I forgot about it, no matter how inconsequential it might have been, I would get upset and self-critical about it. If I were waiting for someone and they were late, even if I was just standing in my house waiting for someone to put on their coat, I would start pacing and become increasingly anxious until I had to wait for them outside.

At first, I just told myself this was normal anxiety, something everyone experiences now and then. But as time went on, these momentary anxieties lasted longer and longer, and grew even more intense. What if my clients began to sense my anxiety? The worry about my worries only made me worry more, and soon my dreams became very intense, very colorful and vivid. I was working with a Jungian therapist, Astara, at the time, so it was natural to focus on them, but the more nervous I became the more the dreams were almost taunting me with their alarming images and I could hardly shake them throughout the day.

In one dream, a nest of snakes had curled around my spinal column, slithering out of my abdomen and turning into butterflies. I watched in perplexed curiosity, more fascinated than horrified. As I thought about the dream throughout the day, I found I was becoming very rattled not by the images as much as by the unrelenting sense that there was something the dream was trying to tell me, something I needed to know about myself or my world that I was just not seeing. But what?

Then suddenly, as if the universe had tried to warn me, my heart was shattered and my world turned upside down. My dear friend Sarah died. I had known her since living in Oregon where we'd been teachers together, and whose hands I held when she gave birth to her first daughter. She had been visiting her family on the east coast when there was a car accident, killing her instantly, and leaving behind her husband and two young daughters, Paulina and Kera.

I was devastated by the news, and my anguish over the little girls who I had known since their births overwhelmed me. I immediately flew to Oregon to be by their side. Over the next few years, I spent as much time playing auntie to these girls as I possibly could. But nothing I could do could possibly replace the tragic loss of their mother, nor could my dear friend ever be replaced.

If the universe had been trying to alert me to tragedy through my dream world, it wasn't through with me. The dreams only intensified, and so, too, did my anxiety. In the corners of my world, I was to discover, someone was waiting for me, someone who would help me make it through the enormous challenge to come.

Crossing the Great Waters

While the sea of milk is being churned,
many good things will come forth.

FROM THE BOOK OF THE BEGINNING
FROM THE MAHABARATA

BY THE TIME my practice was well established, I found myself in my forties, unmarried and childless, the cost many women with careers have had to pay. I had no idea how I had grown into middle age so fast. And while my career was blessed, I seemed to have the opposite gift with love. Every relationship began with so much passion, but that passion soon developed into an unrelenting turbulence that eventually ended the relationship. After a series of failed relationships, I had settled into life as a single woman, dating regularly, getting lots of sexual and romantic attention, but steering clear of getting involved with another man.

But that wasn't the life I wanted. I very much wanted a loving, stable relationship, and I knew that I would never find my center and become a whole person if I didn't find that love. As much as I was drawn to exciting, passionate men, I realized that that kind of guy was just not working out to be a husband. The conventional wisdom says if what you're doing isn't working out, then try something completely different, and this applies to love as much as anything. So if I wanted to find the kind of love that would really center me, I concluded, I needed to shift my view of who was appropriate for me.

Finding that guy was turning out to be harder than I'd ever imagined. I got out as much as I could, travelled and met many interesting men, but there was nothing permanent on the horizon. Then, after a trip to the San Juan Islands with friends, I found myself traveling back on the ferry relaxed and happy, but feeling restless and empty once again to be returning to my single life in Seattle.

"Judith?" The voice was soft and gentle, and I looked up from my seat where I sat, looking out over the water as the soft purple and blues of the islands faded away.

It was Rick, the ski instructor I'd treated in the multi-hands treatment many years before. Rick and I had been bumping into each other frequently over the years, and we always ended up laughing at how often our paths seemed to cross.

Rick was years younger than me, so any thought of romance with him just never crossed my mind, even though I thought he was awfully cute and sweet. In all respects, he was clearly not my type; he was very quiet and reserved and into outdoor sports, and I was pretty artistic and outgoing, quite the opposite. I was more interested in being *in* nature, than running through it! But it sure did energize me to run into him out of the blue like that.

"Rick! What a surprise!" I said, surprising myself by self-consciously standing a bit taller, smoothing my hair, "What are you doing on this ferry? Were you in the San Juans?"

"I'm just coming back from a kayak trip, and I thought I saw you sitting there? What brings you here?" He smiled widely.

We talked about the trips we'd each just had and he asked about my practice and I told him where I was working since the Feldenkrais Center had closed. When the ferry docked, we said good-bye and casually promised to be in touch.

Not long after, Rick began dropping by to see me, and before long, I began to wonder if this young guy was actually flirting with me! At first I thought he was just being sweet, because the more I got to know him, the more clear it was that he was one of the nicest, most sensitive guys I'd ever known. While flirting with a man several years younger had not even crossed my mind, I soon began to wonder if that was, in fact, what we were doing.

"Is that a gray hair?" he said to me one day, with a playful, affectionate smile.

Yes, it turned out it was, and I blushed. Although there wasn't anything the least bit sexual or romantic insinuated by such a simple, innocuous observation, I began to wonder if he might be attracted to me, so I began to ask my friends what they thought.

"Do casual friends—like co-workers or students—ever comment on how you look, or any changes in your appearance, anything like that?" I found myself asking my colleagues whenever we found ourselves chatting casually.

"Like what?" they usually responded.

"You know, like commenting if you had a gray hair or something?"

"Why, did someone say you had gray hair? You look amazing; don't worry about a little gray."

And the conversation would be over.

Or not.

"Oh? Is there someone?" Another might say, mischievously.

"Well, there's this guy, I don't really know him all that well, but . . ." and we would ponder the possibilities, laughing like school girls. The truth was, I was hoping he *was* flirting, but I didn't dare take my fantasies any further than that. He was, after all, seven years my junior.

———

We found ourselves increasingly crossing paths and he began taking classes from me occasionally. After classes, our friendly banter carried on. And we continued to run into each other in unexpected moments, as we had on the ferry. But I kept my distance, because I was a professional and was careful not to cross that line.

The truth was, the closer I got to menopause, the greater my anxiety became, until the periodic anxieties that had troubled me all my life were turning into full-blown panic attacks, and I felt as if I were coming unraveled at any thought of leaving home. I knew this was not the right time to get into a relationship; I needed to figure out what was going on with me and become balanced before I got involved with anyone.

The truth finally hit me like a cyclone one day in the mid-nineties. I had decided to take my late friend Sarah's youngest daughter, Kera, to Indonesia, to visit her older sister. Paulina was by now a teenager and had signed up for a year-long cross-cultural school program in Indonesia, and Kera wanted so badly to join her that I offered to take her for a two week vacation. I'd never been to any place as exotic as Indonesia before and I had always wanted to go. I wanted to help the girls support each other because they had been separated for many months, and I knew that had their mother been alive, she would have made the trip. Also, I was just enchanted at the thought of relaxing in such a calm and tranquil place, where I could enjoy the beautiful art and architecture, eat fabulous feasts, and listen to gamelan, the melodic music of a local orchestra. I had even studied and played in a gamelan group for a few years, enjoying the camaraderie and unusual percussive music of Java and Bali.

The plan was to spend a week in Jogjakarta, a cultural city on the south side of Java where Paulina was living, then another week traveling to Bali, a nearby island. I couldn't imagine a more interesting and restful vacation. But as the trip approached, I started to get very panicky. I just couldn't figure it out; I was so happy to be going, and had no idea why I was becoming so nervous as we got closer to departure. I began having all kinds of racing thoughts, horrible thoughts like what if the plane falls into the sea? How can planes stay up that long going all the way to Asia? It didn't matter that I knew they did it all the time, there was no logic to my thinking; it was just plain panic. What if something happened to Kera? What if we got sick from drinking contaminated water? What if, what if, what if?

I practiced breathing techniques to calm myself, and learned to momentarily control the racing thoughts, but in no time at all they would just rush back at me, like an unrelenting wave of worry. It just got worse and worse and here I was, planning to take charge of a thirteen year old when I couldn't even take care of myself! But thinking like that only made the worries worse. What am I thinking, I'd say to myself, going to a Muslim and Hindu country with two teenage girls, and I'm a single woman? The more I thought about it, the more risky the whole thing seemed, so I went to a pawn shop and bought a gold wedding band.

"There," I said to myself as I slipped it on when I got home, "I'll just wear this and they'll think I'm married and we will travel easily through Java, the Muslim part of Indonesia." Knowing that the there were very different views of unmarried women than I was accustomed to, pretending to be married made me feel safer. I got a whole story in my head about how I was married and who my husband was going to be in case I was ever asked about him so that we could look respectable. I was less concerned about Bali as it was Hindu and a popular international vacation spot. Taking these simple steps seemed to calm me, give me a sense of control over the situation, but not enough control. By the time I got to the airport, I was a nervous wreck. Standing in line with Kera, the reality that I was getting on that plane to fly for hours across an ocean, filled me with an almost crippling fear.

We were standing at the gate when I started to unravel. This occurred well before 9-11 when people could accompany travelers to the gate, so our friend, Kay, had come with us to see us off. Kera was so excited to be going that she was just looking all over the place, not really noticing that I was starting to sweat and shake. But Kay sure noticed it, and the minute I began to hyperventilate, she grabbed me by the arm and whispered forcefully into my ear.

"Judith, stop it! Come on; come with me to the bathroom." Then to Kera she said, "Kera, honey, Judith and I are going to run to the bathroom, you stay right here, okay?"

Oblivious to what was going on with me, Kera said, "Sure, go ahead," then she returned to fiddling with her carry-on bag, making sure she hadn't forgotten anything.

The minute we got into the bathroom, Kay pulled back her hand and slapped me! Just like in the movies. People really do that, it turns out.

"Judith! Get back in your body!" She could see that I was dissociating and that I needed to be present and in better control of myself.

I just stared at her, my panic settling into shock, and I could tell from the look on her face that she was very serious.

"You're getting on that plane and you're going on this trip! Just pull it together!"

I was stunned. Was I really falling apart right there in the airport? Clearly I was or she wouldn't have been so serious, and she sure wouldn't have slapped me. What was going on?

"Okay..." I said, slowly and cautiously. "You're right, I don't know what's going on but I will force myself to act normal." I splashed some water on my face and took some deep breaths until I had some control, and then walked with her back to the gate, repeating to myself, over and over, *breathe in, breathe out, breathe in, breathe out* ... feeling that familiar whisper of air pass through my nostrils.

Somehow, I did it. We got on the plane and I just put myself on automatic, obeying the instructions to fasten our seat belts, making small talk with Kera and flipping nervously through the magazines while focusing on my breath. Inhaling, exhaling, inhaling, exhaling. Gripping the armrests, my head pressed back against the seat, I waited to hit the runway at supersonic speed. As we lifted into the air, I was reciting a Buddhist prayer.

I wished desperately that I had someone by my side that could comfort me, instead of someone who depended on me to comfort her. I looked over at Kera and saw she was so excited, and I smiled and pretended I was, too. And I was, really. But I was so anxious, that it took every bit of my concentration just to keep her from noticing my fear. I knew if she did, that she would become frightened, as well, so I had to just keep breathing deeply and smiling broadly.

All through the long, long flight, I was restless and freezing cold, shifting constantly in my seat, unable to rest, unable to sleep. But I kept myself calm by meditating, and by the time we landed in Jogjakarta, Kera turned to me and said, "I'm so glad you're here, Judith. Every time I woke up in the night, I saw you meditating and then I felt better and went back to sleep. You're so calm."

Boy did that make me want to laugh! I'd never been more agitated in all my life!

Seeing that Kera was calmed by me and hadn't even noticed my panic, gave me the confidence I needed to play auntie and take charge. We were delighted to see Paulina and I was determined that we would have a good trip.

With all my anxiety over all the terrible things that could possibly happen, it had never occurred to me to think about the one thing that is guaranteed to turn any vacation into a test of human strength.

Teenagers.

Paulina and Kera were wonderful girls, and have grown into amazing women, but I had absolutely no experience with being around teenage girls for any length of time, much less in a foreign country, and I soon found I had no idea how to handle two headstrong teenagers.

I wanted to go to every cultural site we could find, both Buddhist and Hindu, and hear the gamelan music and see the art.

They wanted to go shopping.

Worse, when I saw where Paulina was living, I was very upset. There was no host family; she was sixteen, in a foreign country and had absolutely no supervision at all. The government was in a crisis, massive protests were threatening to turn the whole country into a civil war zone, and there was no telling what could happen at any moment. It was so bad, in fact, that there were hardly any tourists; most had sense enough to stay away. Paulina was too young to really appreciate how easily she could have found herself in danger by running around Jogjakarta all by herself. If I'd been her parent, I would have taken her home right then and there, but I wasn't, so I could only counsel her and worry. I even tried persuading her to come home with us, but she wanted to finish the last couple of months in the program, and all I could do was hope that she would be extra careful in the meantime.

Nothing catastrophic happened on the trip. I kept it together, we got home, and Kera never was the wiser to how anxious I'd been. But no sooner did we get back than the government of Indonesia collapsed, and Paulina and her schoolmates were secreted away to the airport in the middle of the night to be flown out of the country to safety. She made it home, safe and sound, and I was tremendously relieved.

But I wasn't so safe or sound. I realized that something was really not right with me and I needed to get some help. Fast. Before my clients realized that I was the one who needed the most healing. And before my brain continued to feel more fractured, with my energy flying in all directions. Somehow, I had to find someone who could help me.

Then, like a broken angel who had fallen at my doorstep, one afternoon I stepped out of my office and saw someone, sitting in the waiting room, squeezing a book of some sort in his hands. He looked completely shattered.

"Rick?" I asked, in disbelief.

"Judith," he said, in visible relief, looking up to me. His eyes were running wet with tears. "I just lost my mother."

"Come on," I said to him, "I think you could use a cup of tea."

———

Rick and I began to have tea together or grab a bite to eat on a regular basis, and were fast becoming good friends, but something still seemed to keep us from taking it any further. After a taco and friendly banter, he'd go off and do his thing and I'd go off and do my thing. But eventually, I knew that he was a man who had captured my heart, and I could tell he felt the same, even if neither of us seemed to have the nerve to take the first step. And Rick was very shy; I knew he wasn't going to make a move anytime soon. So I decided I would.

There was a movie that had just come out about a mountain climbing tragedy on Mount Everest, and I knew that Rick would want to see the movie if he hadn't already seen it.

So one day I asked him, in my most demure manner, "Hey Rick, would you go to that movie with me and explain rock climbing to me?

I'd really like to see it but I'm afraid it won't make any sense to me."

Rick's eyes lit up and he smiled broadly. "Sure," he said, "I'd love to." He later told me he had seen the film already!

So at last, we had a real date. We went to the movie and afterwards he drove me to my car—we lived in different parts of the city so we had met halfway—and we sat together in the front seat with this powerful energy between us, but neither of us said anything at the time. I could tell he wanted to kiss me, but it was still a bit awkward, so we just said goodnight and made another date—for sushi—then went home, both of us feeling incredibly happy.

During the whole sushi dinner, Rick babbled non-stop. If it had been my first encounter with him, I'm not sure what I would have thought, but by then I knew Rick well enough that I could tell he was talking so much because he was incredibly nervous. I just thought to myself, "Wow, this guy must really like me!" And I really liked him; he was such a lovely person and very interesting. He worked as a materials science engineer, and was involved in some confidential project that he couldn't talk about, which made him all the more mysterious and fascinating. He talked and talked about his love of the outdoors, and his heart just seemed to grow bigger and bigger as I got to know him. I'd been with so many men whose hearts were closed or hidden, that finding a man whose sweetness was so deep really appealed to me. I realized I was finally being attracted to the "right" kind of man, a true partner.

Then one evening, I invited him over for dinner. It was Halloween, and maybe that was what led him to think that it was just some casual invitation to drop by, but when he got there, he saw that I had prepared a very nice dinner, with wine.

"Wow!" Rick said when he saw the table set and the candles burning, the kitchen aromatic with several different dishes. "This means something!"

"Yeah, it means something!" I laughed in return, and that was the end of any ambiguity. We made love and he stayed the night, and I realized that unlike with so many other guys, with a guy like Rick it would cement the relationship.

When he left the next morning, I was in heaven. But shortly after, I started having my doubts, wondering if I really wanted to attach myself to anyone. "Do I really want a *relationship* with Rick?" I asked myself, "What if this ruins our friendship? Do I really want to lose that?" I was starting to believe my doubts when I remembered what I'd set out to do in the first place—something different. The relationships I'd had with men had never worked out, so I set out to find a different kind of man and try a different tact. And now here it was, and already I was going back to the same old pattern, asking myself if I really wanted such a sweet guy after all.

"Well you'd better want it," I finally told myself, "Because you got it!" I just opened myself up to being with a wonderful, sweet man, to see where it would take me.

Five years later, it took me to my own backyard, where Rick and I were married. And while my soul had finally found its mate, my brain, it turns out, wasn't quite ready to settle down.

PART
TWO

I attend a Vajrayana retreat with my
spritual teacher, Lama Tsultrim Allione
to learn the Feeding the Demons practice.
I later tell her I am afraid of dying.
She answers that I am afraid of living!

Wind Disturbance

I HAVE ALWAYS hated wind. It is too raw for my skin, too strong as it flows through my body and soul. I cringe and cover my ears with my hands, squint my eyes shut and adjust my oversized scarf to protect my throat, as if the wind could decapitate me with its brutal force. I hate the damage that follows in the wind's path, as it breaks the branches on the stately Douglas Fir trees, tossing them here and there, indiscriminately littering the ground in my garden with limbs that once raised themselves toward the heavens. I carry the remains of a tree once strong and thriving, gently laying the damaged limbs upon a backyard pyre where they will soon turn to rich ash and wandering smoke like a body torn and twisted, dismembered and discarded to return to the earth.

I don't know when or where my fear of the wind began, but one memory still haunts me. It was in the 1970's, when I was young and new to California. I was hiking through the Mojave Desert with Steve, enjoying an almost magical adventure camped on a shapely bluff overlooking the amazing undulating dunes of Death Valley. After a night spent laughing beneath a galaxy of stars, we made our way across those dunes, so gentle from afar, but so difficult to balance upon when underneath our feet.

As the heat grew unrelenting, a strange cloud began to encircle us, the sand suspended in mid-air, growing heavier and heavier until it looked like a thick, swirling carpet about to engulf us. Suddenly, as we struggled to move through the thickening, rising sand, a fierce wind storm struck, blowing great gales of stinging, suffocating sand with a violent force as if it sought only to destroy us. We had no choice but to go on across the windy plains to the car parked in a distant canyon, the cutting sand lashing our faces without mercy. Like soldiers crossing the Sahara we marched on, one foot in front of the other, sand in my mouth, my pack getting heavier each hour. It was unendurable, but I wouldn't give up, as the heat roasted our flesh and the vicious sand sliced our faces and bare hands with every step. We moved through the sandstorm for what felt like hours, and when we finally reached our yellow Volkswagen bug we were elated! It was more wondrous than a stretch limousine waiting at the curb—at last, we were saved!

We raced to the car and slammed the doors shut, brushing the sand from our faces, our hair, our ears, our noses and eyes and our clothes. The sand, now in every crevice and fiber of our flesh and clothing, was everywhere, coating us like sandpaper. But at least we were out of the deathly storm, safe in our little shelter.

And the car wouldn't start.

"What do you mean the car won't start?" I cried out, incredulously, "It's a Volkswagen! It can't die!"

"It may not be dead, but it sure is in a deep coma" Steve said, puzzled, shaking his head. "There must be sand in the engine."

We were doomed. The car was so stifling hot it felt as if we'd be cremated alive, while outside the sandstorm continued to howl violently, whipping the sands into suffocating clouds blowing across the horizon. If we got back out we'd be sandblasted to death, I was certain. Then it began to rain mud; big, dark blobs splattered on the windshield in rapid succession.

The only thing to do was laugh. The irony got the best of us, turning our traumatic adventure into a hilarious one. Fortunately, we were in a national park, and not the Sahara, so we knew we would probably be saved before we were baked alive or buried underneath a dune of sand. Sure enough, a few minutes later, a car miraculously appeared in the distance, driving along the sandy dirt road straight toward us like a wondrous mirage. They helped us clean the engine and start the car; at last we were saved!

We drove out of there in good spirits, but the seriousness of the situation didn't escape me. I now knew the wind to be a force to contend with. And I knew I could survive.

—

Now, years later, I again felt threatened by a strong wind, and my survival in the face of its fury seemed a lifetime ago. As I grew older, my self-confidence had matured and I was now married and well established in my career, I felt calm and centered in my life's direction. Yet curiously, as I became more centered in my life, a vague and perplexing anxiety, a sense of constant dread, seemed to creep up and overwhelm me with a mind and a timing of its own.

Over time, this anxiety turned to fear, not of the wind or nature, but of an unnamed calamity. My fears moved from the elements, to the elemental—if I drove somewhere, the car could crash; if I left the house, the house could burn. My mind seemed to leap immediately from a place of comfort and safety, to one of danger, fixated on every conceivable thing that could go wrong in daily life. I could only boil it down to the fear of dying and I couldn't fathom exactly why.

At first, when the anxiety would build, I told myself it wouldn't last. And in most cases it did not. Not at first. The panic attack at the airport seemed as if it would be just an isolated event in my life. Soon after Rick and I were married, my menopause began, and the changes in my hormones hit me hard. The once vague and almost distant anxiety seemed to take root and grow, entwining my nervous system like strangling tendrils. I knew I had to do something to change it.

I noticed the panic began to return almost anytime I felt a slight bit of stress. It became more and more debilitating and irrational, erupting over nothing at all. Rick would go skiing and I would be twisting my hands in worry until he returned. Just the thought of leaving the house could trigger a crescendo of panic symptoms, fixing me in place rather than risk the calamities outside my door—if I drove for groceries, I might get a flat tire, and find myself stranded in the middle of nowhere. If I walked to the park, I could be attacked by a dog. If I got into a friend's car, they might lose control and we'd crash. The endless possibilities of disasters awaiting me outside my door flashed through my brain like a never-ending nightmare. I would get shaky and cold and hear whooshing in my ears. My emotions were reacting in a roaring river of thoughts. I tried to observe them, quietly trying to control their speed, but the accompanying body-felt sensations overwhelmed me, pushing me to scream or cry with a blanket pulled over my head.

I had survived crossing through a sandstorm in Death Valley, and being stranded in one of the hottest places on earth, and come out laughing. I had survived two decades of adulthood as a single woman, establishing a successful practice and career, all by myself. I had survived relationship break-ups, cross-country moves, and even graduate school, and never felt any fear like this. Now here I was in middle age, nearly paralyzed by the thought of driving to the store. It made no sense to my rational mind. It was utter madness and it was eating me alive. I did everything possible to appear normal on the outside, at peace with the world and in my life, but I was really terrified that if my clients sensed the nervousness within me, they would leave—and just the thought of that happening could send my mind on one of its wild thought patterns into certain doom. It turned out I could control its outside appearance fairly well.

It was remarkable how well I hid the intensifying anxiety from my clients, but somehow, I managed to carry on with my work as if everything were normal. Clearly the years of training and practice helped me. It helped that my clients lay on a table with their eyes closed while I worked, grounded into the earth as was my habit. But it was becoming very difficult to hide my panic attacks from my friends, and impossible to conceal my state from my husband.

———

Marriage had come to me, and to Rick, late in our lives, but we found that it suited us remarkably well. As with anyone, there were many adjustments to be made, but we quickly found a balance between respecting each other's autonomy and giving each other support. As the unrelenting waves of anxiety became harder and harder to shake, I began to fear Rick would realize how flawed and weak I truly was, and so I tried even harder to conceal it from him. Somehow I managed to mask the panic when it came to daily life, finding excuses for why I couldn't get to the store, explaining the obvious signs of worry when he was leaving for work as having something else on my mind that was making me appear so agitated. (He later told me he had seen right through me and simply tried to be there for me, though at the time, he never said a word.) When he suggested a trip to Baja, and I reluctantly agreed, I found I could no longer hide how hellish the panic attacks had become once we arrived in the desert by the sea.

We left at the end of June, a time when it was very hot in Mexico. I had become very uncomfortable with heat once menopause commenced, finding it increased my bodily discomfort. I was having a terrible time with the hot flashes, which came suddenly and left slowly, making me feel feverish and desperate for cool air.

I breathed rhythmically and deeply all the way to the airport and onto the plane, meditating silently as we flew to Mexico. But when we got off the plane in Cabo San Lucas and walked across the street to rent a car, ten days of pure panic and hell began. The furnace of air was already distressing me, compressing my body from every angle. Every moment I could find to cool myself was an ecstatic moment—a sip of juice, a splash of water on my face, a moment underneath a whirring fan, a step inside an air-conditioned building.

We drove north in a tiny rental car to the village of Todos Santos. Todos Santos is a cute little town that I would have been thrilled to visit in the past, but with the tidal waves of fear taking hold of me, I was only distracted. No matter what I did, I just couldn't calm myself down long enough to linger anywhere. My mind would create any trauma that could happen, based on anything I saw or anywhere I was. Was the car too small? Would it die as we crossed those hot plains, like the Volkswagen's death by the sandstorm? Would the cool watery waves of the ocean kill us both with a rogue wave swallowing us up like a tsunami?

My thoughts created a catastrophic threat around every situation we were in. I was constantly worrying, worrying and worrying that something horrible would surely happen on our trip. And when it didn't happen, my mind would jump to the next imaginary event that I knew with absolute certainty was going to happen. I was so convinced our fate was sealed if we remained in Todos Santos, that I couldn't wait to get out of there. I couldn't explain my fears to Rick, I couldn't let him know how tormented I truly was. This was our vacation; he'd brought me to Baja to relax! But the last thing I could do was relax amidst all the potential disasters.

"I don't know what it is about this place, Rick," I explained to him, "I just have a really bad feeling about it."

"Okay," he said, cheerily, "Why don't we go to La Paz? It's a small town near here, and it's supposed to be very charming."

"Okay," I said agreeably, breathing deeply to calm myself, "I'm willing to trust a town whose name means Peace."

And so we drove to La Paz, but we had barely even entered the town when we got a flat tire. Rick was clearly frustrated as the car hobbled to the side of the road and he got the jack and spare tire out of the trunk. But I was practically jubilant by the event. Finally, a calamity had happened! Somehow I found it more calming to actually have something bad happen, than to live with the anxiety of what could possibly happen.

Rick put on the spare tire and we drove to a tire store in La Paz, where I was thrilled to stay inside the air-conditioned building and watch a soccer game on a small TV. Any cool room that we stayed in was heavenly for me because it reduced my body temperature to a manageable state. However, after we left the store and wandered around La Paz, I didn't find anything the least bit peaceful about it. Walking on the hot streets, the anxiety and agitation came creeping back, and before long, I was begging Rick to hit the road again.

So we drove to a small and beautiful village by the sea, Cabo Pulmo, to relax for five days. That's when the panic really started to hit me! I found it ironic that trying to relax was causing me so much anxiety, but the more anxious I felt, the more my thoughts raced, and the more my thoughts raced, the more anxious I felt. I would get so hot that I would want nothing more than to cool down in the sea. I would wade into the sea, but the minute the water lapped my calves and moved up my thighs I would panic. The water felt too cold, too deep, too murky, too something. Tiny colorful fish tickled my legs as they brushed against my skin, and I felt as if an anaconda was about to swallow me. The image became so real I couldn't shake it.

Years before I'd had a dream that I was crossing a bridge over murky water when an anaconda suddenly sprang out of the water and wrapped itself tightly around me, pulling me back into its watery lair. The dream had had such a powerful impact on me that I'd remembered it all these years, and now that I was wading in the sparkling turquoise sea, the night-mare had come to life, perhaps aided by the image of the tentacles of an octopus, Cabo Pulmo's namesake. In the dream, however, I loosened myself from the anaconda and escaped. Here I wasn't so sure I could escape the panic.

I would swim for a few moments, and then I'd begin to panic. Getting out of the water, I would persuade Rick to return to our little bungalow, where we would climb up and into our little stork's nest lookout to gaze at the sea. There, perched high above the white sandy beach, I somehow felt safer, protected from the dangers that surely awaited us below. I had no fear of heights. When I felt calm enough to return to the water, the panic would set in again and I'd want only to return to the bungalow.

At night, I took medication to sleep, because I knew I had to have some rest. I just wanted to enjoy my vacation. I had always been wary of pharmaceutical medications, but this time I had no other choice.

Through it all, Rick was so understanding, though clearly confused, wondering why I was so worried. Unbelievably, I somehow managed to appear far less crazy on the outside than I was feeling on the inside. He intuitively sensed that something wasn't right, and he took wonderful care of me, cooling my face with wet cloths and bringing me cool juices to drink.

The nights in Cabo Pulmo were really horrible because our little thatched hut was very, very hot. We slept with soaking wet cloths laid across our chests and necks, with the fans aimed straight at us, humming us to sleep. But neither of us could really sleep very long. We would get up in the middle of the night and take cool showers, stumbling back to bed to try to catch a few hours of rest before morning. The whole trip was anything but relaxing; it was utterly exhausting!

The entire trip felt like I was reliving my birth, smothered by the suf-focating heat, terrified of what was happening to me. My body seemed to have an agenda all its own, for no matter how much I would talk myself through each terrifying moment, tell myself it wasn't real, that I was safe and protected, I succumbed to shaking, shivering from the chills, my skin crawling as if I were covered head to toe with insects, followed by heat-searing hot flashes. By the time we got on the plane to go home I was as relieved as if we'd escaped from the bowels of Hell itself.

—

Rick and I were forced to fly back sitting in different parts of the plane because it was so crowded, but I didn't mind that at all. I was just so relieved to be going home. It felt safe to return home and I began to calm down. The flight was uneventful for the most part and I just dozed. Then at one point I looked out the window and saw that we were flying over Crater Lake in Oregon. My mind fell far down into the crater, tumbling and falling into the darkness of the crater, and I suddenly had a vivid image of myself flying in a spaceship over the earth, watching a legendary island explode into a kaleidoscope of fiery fragments beneath me. The image was so vibrant, so real, that it felt more like a memory than my imagination. I sat trembling on the airplane as the sensation of watching the explosion took hold of me, and I rapidly made notes in my dream journal because seeing these images was just like a dream. I began to wonder about anxiety and the images that come with it. What are its causes? How does it decide to manifest itself through one's mind? Why was it gripping me with such tenacious force? What was it trying to tell me?

These questions flooded my thoughts all the way home, and I knew I had to find some answers. But first I had to calm myself down. So, as soon as we reached home and were settled, I called Karen, my friend and colleague in CranioSacral therapy, imploring her to fit me into her schedule.

"Of course, Judith, I can see you tomorrow afternoon. Is that soon enough?" she asked me.

"Yes!" I answered, "I'll be there!"

That night, I rested peacefully beside Rick, so happy to be home where I felt safe. However, the next day, as I was driving to see Karen, I began having another panic attack, a full blown attack that was far, far worse than anything I'd experienced in Mexico, as horrifying as that experience had been.

I began shaking as my mind started screaming at me, thoughts careening through my head telling me that I was no good, crazy, falling apart. Crazy thoughts hammered away at me in a harsh, mean-spirited script that ran through my head like an abusive guardian. I became very angry, furious at the panic that was ruling my life, destroying my life, just when I'd found everything I'd always wanted—a home, a fantastic career, and a wonderful, loving husband.

"Stop it!! Leave me alone!!" I raged at the panic, as if it were a demon that had possessed me. I pulled the car over onto a side street and started screaming and screaming as I squeezed the steering wheel in a white-knuckled grip.

"Stop it! Stop it! Stop it!" I screamed at the demons that possessed me. *"Leave me alone! Just leave me alone!"* I cursed and swore, screaming an avalanche of obscenities at the demonic panic, and then suddenly everything went instantly quiet. I couldn't believe it. There was nothing but silence and dead calm inside my head. What had happened? Had I chased the panic demons away once and for all? With all my training I had never thought to yell at them. I smiled.

I drove to Karen's and lay down on the table and we worked. In our minds we connected with the goal of using golden light from the heavens to heal me, and it was a very peaceful treatment. Her hands cradled my head and neck and calmed my mind and body with their touch. Later she held my sacrum with one hand and another hand on my abdomen.

When I got up from the table, I felt immensely better, but I knew it wasn't over. I drove home carefully, in peace, as I focused on the light, saying prayers to Green Tara, the protector. It was early July, and very warm, a healing warmth, and I inhaled its healing powers.

When I got home, rather than go inside, something told me to go into the backyard and lie down on the warm earth. I lay on the ground and started uncontrollably shaking; I just shook and shook and shook like a trembling child. When I was calmer, Rick helped me inside and we talked about my increasing anxiety. I had been so afraid that if he knew how uncontrollable the anxiety was becoming, that he would think he had married a lunatic, but he was so incredibly caring and concerned that telling him brought me a wonderful sense of calm and safety.

I spent much of the next three days just lying on the ground in our garden, shaking. It felt good to be on the earth. The earth supported my body. I felt it was the right thing to do, a Reichian discharge of energy perhaps. It was warm in the shade and Rick worked on a project nearby. After three days, my body was calm. The shaking, the trembling, the absolute fear were absorbed by the earth. I felt jubilant! I felt very self-assured, and cured. I had somehow intuitively solved the anxiety by listening to my body's need to shake. My body was teaching me what I needed so desperately to know—it contained the answers to its own suffering, inside it all along.

—

I later found a passage in *Taking the Leap* (2009), a book by Pema Chodron, a Tibetan Buddhist teacher:

> A few years ago I was overwhelmed by deep anxiety,
> a fundamental, intense anxiety with no storyline
> attached. I felt very vulnerable, very afraid and raw.

While I sat and breathed with it, the terror did not abate, and I didn't know what to do…I went to see my teacher and he said, "Oh, I know that place… that's the Dakini Bliss. That's a high level of spiritual bliss…(that comment) completely changed the way I looked at it.

Reading this gave me a lot to think about. I read and reread this many times, puzzling over her experience compared to mine.

Riding on the Tail
of the Tiger

Ophiuchus, the serpent slayer and healer,
is the name of an ancient constellation of
a man grasping a snake while stepping on
a scorpion. It represents Asclepius, the
healer who learned the secrets of keeping
death at bay after observing one serpent
bringing another some healing herbs.

PERSONAL CONVERSATION
WITH AN ASTROLOGER

THE ANXIETY WAS gone, and my life was finally at peace. For months,
I felt normal again, and my career and marriage to Rick thrived. I was
now working from my home studio full time, and I felt more centered
and calm than I had ever been before. The inexplicable urge to lie on
the ground and shake, I had come to learn, was a primal response that
helped me to recover.

Somatic therapist Peter Levine writes that animals, in a state of
terror, will freeze to protect themselves and tremble to recalibrate the
nervous system. Drawing on his studies of how traumatized animals self-
heal, Levine encourages a natural arising of the therapeutic response

of shaking to discharge trauma. In other words, my body instinctively responded by self-healing in its primal state, as I literally "shook off" the fears and anxieties that haunted me. Dr. Bruno Chikly, in his Brain Curriculum, calls the same process "down-regulating" the nervous system and has taught his students how to accomplish the same effect using touch with clients.

However, I feared that the anxiety would return, so I made sure to take care of my body. For decades I had taken homeopathic and acupuncture treatments, and I continued these diligently. I also resumed seeing Astara, the Jungian analyst I had known for twenty years; she helped me through the difficult struggles of building a career and helped me through so many relationships with family, friends and men.

When I first started seeing Astara two decades prior, she invited me to our first session and asked me to bring a dream. That same night I woke up in terror, drenched in sweat. I had dreamt that the face of a giant vampire with bright eyes and sharp teeth was staring straight at me, just inches from my own face. I was completely terrified, but I dutifully wrote down the dream and went back to sleep. Then I had another dream, a much more peaceful dream. I was standing in a river with Steve, the man from the desert sandstorm trip, we were in love. We were dressed in wedding clothes and hugging each other, and I felt very complete, very whole.

When I woke up, I wondered who this man could be, for Steve was married and lived elsewhere. I wrote down the dream and the next day took it to my first session with her.

Astara analyzed the vampire dream as the anxiety and the wedding dream as the goal. "This is what we're going to work on," she told me, "the unification of the whole person."

I loved that approach, and began seeing her regularly. Then, after Rick and I married, I stopped seeing her for several years. I felt that since partnership was the issue we'd been working on all those years that I didn't need her anymore. But following the panic attacks, I knew I needed as much help as I could get, and I went back to her until the panic attacks finally subsided. She encouraged me to face the fears and understand that it was the body expressing anxiety through sensations, expressing it and releasing it.

I was very productive and thriving once the attacks stopped, but after about a year, ever so slowly, they started to creep into my life again. It started with my sleep. I noticed that I slept a lot; I was such a workaholic that I was terribly exhausted by the end of the day and would come home and crash. After marrying Rick, I cut back on the busy work schedule and had a lot more energy. As the anxiety began to creep in, I got to the point where I was really having a terrible time falling asleep. I was completely exhausted but every night I laid in bed, with my thoughts racing practically all night. Springtime came and the birds were singing and new sprouts shooting up from the earth and the temperature warming, but the wind felt cold. The wind cut through my skin and chilled my soul, as if sending gusts of anxiety through me with every breeze. I still so feared the wind.

I feared, too, that I would disappear. I began to wonder what would happen if I actually *did* disappear. Of course, nothing actually would happen because I would be disappeared, poof, gone in an instant, and my ego along with me. It seemed like it would be a good thing, and that is as close as I came to desiring death. What actually disappears? I began to wonder.

"Abandonment and annihilation are primordial fears," Astara explained, "Fear of disappearing is about object constancy. Just as the baby wants to be comforted, the body becomes the stand-in for the baby."

I reflected on these fears and worries, spending more and more time with them, as the anxiety began returning. It seemed like normal stuff at first. I would find myself worrying more over money, worrying over my practice, worrying more as I began to gain weight following menopause; just the ordinary worries of daily living. But the worries intensified, and eventually, I had to accept that they were not normal worries at all, but signs that the anxiety was returning. I was so groggy all the time, so very exhausted, that the slightest sensation in my body felt overpowering. I had weird sensations all over my body, and they grew more and more unnerving. At the same time, I began to lose all motivation. I could not make the simplest of decisions, because I found myself obsessing over them until I was virtually paralyzed by fear, a fear that I could feel deep into my brainstem, shaking my body's core.

Strangely, I developed an obsessive desire to crunch something with my teeth. I had a constant craving for crunchy food, like nuts or popcorn, anything hard and brittle that I could crush between my teeth. I would enter into such a fierce state that crunching seemed like the only thing I could do to alleviate an overwhelming desire to bite down. I wanted to bite anything—or anyone. I just wanted to attack, to kill, to somehow savagely tear into people, into things, to absolutely destroy. I was literally experiencing the vampire dream!

I could no longer hide the fact that I was losing control. I knew that Rick was not leaving me, but his commitment did nothing to calm me and that really surprised me—to realize that even the nurturing love of a partner could not bring me peace. My friends urged me to seek help, yet I felt so all alone, as if no one was there for me. I felt so desperate for help, and so abandoned.

And where would I go for help anyway, I wondered. I was already under the care of many practitioners—body workers, a homoeopath, an acupuncturist, a naturopathic physician and a primary care physician. They all did everything they could to help me—they gave me herbs, hormones, manipulations. Nothing worked.

One physician advised me that anxiety has a life of its own.

"I can't tell you what will happen," she said, "Prepare for the unknown. You have all the tools you need."

The unknown? That was precisely what was bringing on the panic attacks. I didn't want to hear that. I wanted answers, not more mysteries.

"I can't live like this," I told her, "I need to know what's happening to me, it's the unknown that's so terrifying."

"Your body is changing," she explained, "and you need to stay in relationship with the parts of your body during the process. Your body is telling you to prepare for this journey of aging."

Her voice was so soothing, and her explanation sort of made sense, but still I was terrified. I just didn't feel strong enough to continue without help. It just seemed as if all the healers and practitioners I saw listened to me but didn't really suggest anything specific that I should do besides continue with acupuncture, herbs, meditation and my work with Astara. Those were my preferred methods of treatment, but they weren't working. The anxiety was only getting worse, worse than it had ever been.

By late spring of 2008 I was a nervous wreck. I was too thin, vibrating so much I was losing a pound a day. I was exhausted but could barely sleep and when I did I was tormented by nightmares.

"I've been having all kinds of crazy dreams," I told Astara, "and now I've started having dreams of being attacked by knives: steel knives and crystal knives. If I even see a knife or a rack of knives I get shaky. I've never had any problem with knives before, what's that all about?"

I tried laughing at the absurdity of my mounting phobias, but I couldn't hide my fear. She knew me too well, and she knew that whatever was going on with me, it was something really big.

"These are primordial fears," she told me. "They're ancestral fears, the fear that you will not survive."

"Okay, I see," I said, starting to understand, "but what does that have to do with knives?"

"Knives are a weapon; they can annihilate your ego and you are resisting."

I was unconvinced. I thought about the knife of the dakinis and the practices Lama Tsultrim had taught me for cutting the ego. "It's like I've had some terrible trauma associated with knives, but that doesn't make any sense at all."

"These panic attacks you've been having are preverbal memories that you've kept bottled inside you all these years. You've been so focused on healing your body from these attacks, that your mind is telling you to stop and pay attention to what you've forgotten."

I thought about what she said for a moment. All through the winter I had caught myself looking up to the magnetic knife holder hanging over our kitchen sink and sensing danger. I would practically feel the sharp edges of the knives with my gaze, and feel afraid. I had never before perceived them as dangerous. They were tools I used for cutting vegetables and meat. But suddenly, over the winter they seemed to change. They looked very harmful and I knew I had to stay away. It wasn't like I was going to kill myself or anybody else for that matter, but for some inexplicable reason after hanging there for years, the knives had suddenly become ominous.

And then I remembered. Just as Astara had said, I had completely forgotten a terrible event from my childhood, as if I had purposefully buried it so that I wouldn't have to ever recall it again.

I was young and we were living in our old house, the one we had before moving to Scarsdale. My sister and I used to play under the formal dining room table. We liked to turn the dark wooden table into a hiding place, with the dark blue carpet beneath us and the dark blue coverings of the chairs enveloping us like a comforting sea where the world was safe and magical and grownups couldn't reach us.

I remembered crouching under the table with her one time, but we weren't playing. Our parents were having a terrible fight in the kitchen, yelling at each other so loudly that we were petrified. The kitchen was right next to the dining room, so we had a clear view of their argument, while we huddled together under the table.

My mother was holding a shiny silver knife—a big kitchen knife—and she was pointing it right at my father and screaming in rage. I was terrified she would kill him.

I related my memory, my voice shaking. And when I'd finished telling it, I felt this incredible sense of calm. It was as if the memory has washed a wave of calmness over me, and I felt tremendously relieved.

Astara smiled, a gentle, peaceful smile.

"Once again you are loosening the grip of the mother complex within," she explained. "And you are getting better."

But I wasn't getting better. My fear of knives vanished, but the anxieties and panic attacks persisted. I needed help, I realized. Serious help.

A Moon in Cancer

I see illnesses as sorrows of the soul.

EMILIE CONRAD

"I'M AFRAID YOU have cancer."

The gynecologist's words left me stunned. I didn't hear anything after that, not for a few moments at least, as I tried to process what she had said. She had fit me into her busy schedule for an emergency biopsy after an ultrasound had revealed suspicious growths in my uterus. Being postmenopausal, when I began spotting blood, I knew something was wrong so I had arranged for the ultrasound, confident at the time that I was just being properly cautious. Oddly, I hadn't panicked when I noticed the bleeding. My practitioner training kicked in, and I just did what needed to be done to be sure my body was alright. And that meant getting the ultrasound. Which, it turned out, meant hearing the gynecologist say the deathly word. Cancer.

I wished I had brought Rick along with me; what was I thinking? I was terrified of driving to the store, yet for some reason I had driven to the hospital all by myself. Now I sat on the edge of a cold exam table, dressed only in a flimsy gown, as the physician matter-of-factly pronounced my insides cancerous. There was nothing at all soothing about her tone; she spoke, in a hurried tone, as if she was rushing to get to her next uterus. I wanted her to soften the words, but she was so direct that

113

her words felt harsh and punishing.

"Of course we won't know for sure until we do a biopsy and I have a chance to review the results," she said rapidly, "but your uterine lining is 11 millimeters thick, which is very suspicious. Until it's proven otherwise by a negative biopsy, I'm going to err on the side of caution."

"What's that mean?" I asked her, my knuckles whitening as I tightly gripped the stirrups on either side of the exam table.

"It means I'm going to assume you have cancer until I know otherwise. Now lean back and let's take a look at your cervix."

She had to tell me to relax several times; I was so frightened that my entire abdomen was a giant knot of tension. "Since you've never had a child, your cervix is very narrow," she said, almost to herself as I felt her hands poking and prodding my interior. "I may not be able to do a biopsy today; we may have to schedule a D&C for another day. If we find cancer, we're going to have to do a complete hysterectomy and then. . ."

But I didn't hear much of what she was saying. Every word that came out of her mouth sent me into a greater state of panic, but I was still lying on the exam table half naked under the harsh glare of the fluorescent lights. I knew I needed to stay calm and preserve my dignity. I used all my skills to relax my cervix so that she could do the biopsy. I felt myself dissociate from the fear to relax the tissues, while with incredible precision, the doctor managed to insert her tools up my vaginal walls and into my cervix, and did the biopsy. Then she stood up and peeled off her latex gloves, tossing them in the trash as she picked up her pen and began scribbling away, talking as she did so about returning the following week to get the test results, never once looking at me. She left the exam room abruptly, obviously rushing to get to her next patient.

I got off the exam table and stood up to dress, but as soon as I did, I started feeling faint. I lay on the cool floor to rest and passed out.

I awoke as a nurse was gently helping me to my feet. She took care of me and assured me she'd follow up with the results as soon as they were available. I couldn't imagine waiting an entire week, not knowing if I were dying or not.

The next day, the doctor called me at home.

"I have good news," she said, and proceeded to tell me the tests were negative for cancer. It was a phone call from heaven; I forgave her for all her harsh and abrupt demeanor, I was so elated to hear her voice now.

"But I still want to force a bleed to clean out your uterus," she said as I was still playing her words of salvation in my head: "You don't have cancer."

Force a bleed? Images of blood gushing all over the place flooded my brain. I paced around the house frantically as the gynecologist talked on the phone. My thoughts cascaded into a frenzy of anxiety, and I was doing everything possible to keep it together. I asked her which hormones were causing the anxiety.

"You need to calm down," she told me in her direct, no-nonsense voice, "your anxiety is not caused by your hormones. It's caused by something else."

Hearing her say those words shocked me. Of course it was my hormones. What else could it be? The panic attacks started after menopause, and that's when my hormone levels changed so drastically.

"That doesn't mean the hormonal changes have caused your anxiety," she said, "You need to see another specialist for that. In the meantime, I want to force a bleed because your uterine lining has gotten too thick." She put me on a course of strong progesterone so I had a period and sloughed off some uterine lining. And she warned me to stay away from estrogen, a potential cause of the growth.

The "big bleed" that I was dreading turned out to be just a few drips. That seemed to be enough to satisfy her and the problem seemed resolved. The uterine bleeding stopped and I did not need surgery.

However, it wasn't resolved for me, and I was determined to do whatever I could to figure out how to get my uterine lining to shrink so that it didn't turn into cancer later on.

I went to an herbalist, and she recommended an environment that was free of estrogenic substances. She gave me a list of products I needed to avoid like pesticides, plastics, perfumes, and nail polish. I already knew about those toxins but I realized there were foods to avoid, like soy products and herbs with estrogenic properties so I had to read label ingredients carefully.

Finally, I made an appointment with a physician I trusted completely to deal with the anxiety. I preferred to avoid allopathic medical doctors, and in this case I was avoiding a psychiatrist, choosing a familiar physician. After all, alternative medicine wasn't alleviating the panic attacks, and if it wasn't hormones, what was it that was causing me to live in such a perpetual state of fear?

The physician prescribed a popular anti-depressant, and I dutifully filled the prescription and went home. Although the wisdom in my body kept shouting *"No!"* I took the pill obediently. How could I tell the difference between "my" anxiety and my body's wisdom? I didn't notice much the first time I took it, or the second, but the third time I took it with much trepidation. The moment the pill went into my mouth I knew it was a huge mistake. My body reacted very strongly against it and within an hour, I found myself in the midst of the most horrifying panic attack of my life, an attack that lasted not the customary hour or two, but eight hours of sheer panic.

I thought I was losing my mind, but I also knew that whatever was happening to me was a reaction to the drug. Back in the 1970's I had experimented with the drugs of the era—mild in comparison to the recreational drugs of today—so I knew that I could talk myself through this drug reaction and that it would end when enough hours passed for my body to excrete it. But I must say that day was pure hell. The somatic experience of having a drug-induced panic attack was beyond anything I'd ever had before.

My mind was running in two dozen directions, my body was shaking and I was freezing cold. Worst of all, I was working. I had taken the medicine shortly before going to work, and found the panic overtaking me while I was working on a client. I focused all my powers on exerting a tremendous amount of mental control, granting my hands the power that my altered brain had lost. I let my hands do all the work as they moved across the client's body, touching, palpating, manipulating. I silently heard Astara saying to me, "you will always be able to work," and recalling her words, I felt calmer. I let the words become my prayer or mantra, letting the phrase run again and again through my head as my hands worked, and I battled to control my racing mind.

Astara had been right. I was able to work—even when I was shaking inside, I was able to move through my work; my body knowledge had taken over.

The medication finally wore off late in the day. I cancelled my clients and spent the next few days just resting and feeling very nervous, wondering what to do next, where to turn.

Finally, one of my good friends suggested that if I was going to mess around with my brain chemistry, I should see a professional. I knew she was right, in fact, I thought it was a great idea. Despite having such a bad experience with that first medication, I knew that there was something wrong with my physiology and alternative treatments just hadn't helped. I had to have some kind of medication if only to help get me to a place where I could function well enough to allow other treatments to work.

So she put me in touch with a nurse practitioner—a nurse who could prescribe medications. I thought seeing a nurse practitioner might be better than seeing a psychiatrist, because nurses are more likely to spend time talking with their patients and finding out what is really going on. I made an appointment for a few days later and let me tell you, those few days were tortuous. The anxiety continued to express itself somatically: uncontrollable shaking, inability to be still, thoughts racing, nearly unable to speak coherently. I was really falling apart.

The appointment wasn't until later in the day, and just the thought of going was making me frantic. What would happen? What if she put me on a powerful medication that caused even more problems? What if she had no idea what to do to help me? What if she gave me bad advice? The "what ifs" began swirling through my head until I couldn't think straight. I went into the backyard and began to pull weeds, and activity that seemed to keep me somewhat focused as my body shook uncontrollably. I kept shaking my hands and wrists as if they'd been contaminated with something, shaking and shaking to release the blocked energy, until finally I couldn't even pull up weeds. I went back in the house and begged Rick to take me to a psychiatric hospital.

"I don't know what's wrong with me, but I just can't take this anymore, Rick!" I cried. "My whole nervous system is *fried!*" I just wanted so badly to feel normal, to feel calm and protected. And I could tell that Rick was beside himself watching me lose all control, and knowing that no matter what he did, nothing helped me.

"You're going to make it, Judith," he assured me in a calm voice, "You don't need to go to a psychiatric hospital. You need to see the nurse. Let's just hold on until we get there, okay?"

"Okay," I answered nervously, "but if I can't make it, you have to promise me you'll take me to a hospital."

"I promise," he said, and he held me tightly, rocking me gently until I was calm enough to make it through the day.

When I saw the nurse, she diagnosed me with a high-level anxiety disorder resulting from a lack of sleep. So I wasn't crazy, I just had insomnia!

It was true; I hadn't slept more than a few hours a night in two years.

"I'm going to prescribe tranquilizers," she told me, in a comforting but authoritative tone. Tranquilizers. The very thought of them brought back memories of the early 1960's and "mother's little helper," the drug of choice for housewives.

"You mean for the panic attacks?" I said, assuming she meant that I take them whenever I found myself spinning out of control.

"Yes, I want you to take them once a day for a month," she said.

"Every day? For a month?" She wanted me to be tranquilized constantly! I felt so ashamed. Me, the hippie alternative medicine girl, taking tranquilizers! But I was so desperate that if she'd have prescribed rattlesnake venom I'd have taken it.

"Yes, we need to get you sleeping on a regular schedule before we do more, so I'd like to start with this. Depending on how you do with the tranquilizers, we can transition you off to something milder."

"Like what?" I asked.

"There are a number of medications, but we'll start with something tried and true to treat the anxiety."

"So I won't be on these tranquilizers after a month?" I asked, still worried I might end up on them long term.

"No, I promise you, we'll get you off. I can't say how long, but it won't be long, just enough to get you sleeping more regularly."

Calmed by her assurances that I wouldn't be on tranquilizers the rest of my life, I left feeling hopeful. Rick drove me to a pharmacy where I filled the prescription and took the prescribed dose, and I went home to see what it felt like to be tranquilized. But nothing happened. Two hours later I was still wide awake and as nervous as ever. So I called her and told her they had done nothing to help me at all.

"Please, can't you prescribe something else?" I pleaded, hoping she'd realize that I wasn't a tranquilizer kind of girl.

"No, let's give these a try first. Just take another pill and see how you do with a higher dose."

I did, and fell into a very deep sleep. I slept all through the rest of the afternoon, the evening and all through the night. I hadn't really slept in years and by the time I woke up I felt so much more rested and happy to have finally fallen asleep.

That first month of taking the tranquilizers changed my state of mind immensely. I felt calmer and more relaxed than ever before, and when I returned to see her each week throughout that month I felt like a completely different person. I still didn't want to keep taking the tranquilizers, but I was much more agreeable to them now that I saw how much they helped me. Instead, we decided that I would transition to a mild anti-anxiety medication.

I took those for about nine months, and during that time there was no nervousness, no panic, and no anxiety. It was an interesting time, because I felt as if I'd finally gained control over my demons—but I was too drugged and slowed down to really function at the level I was used to. It was as if I had swapped one demon for another, and in that drugged state, I knew I had only managed to cover up the anxiety, not eradicate it. I felt calm, but I sure didn't trust this calmness because I could sense the anxiety demon down deep inside me, lurking in some crevice of my soul or nervous system, hiding and waiting, like the anaconda in my dreams of many years ago. It, too, was waiting silently in the slimy muck, and now I finally felt as if I understood what that dream had been trying to tell me all along. Something huge and dangerous was awaiting me, something really big, but I didn't dare think about it too much, because I didn't want to let that demon loose again. Still, I felt that I needed to do something to prevent it from growing. I knew I didn't want to live the rest of my life in a drugged state anymore than I wanted to live the rest of my life in a state of constant panic.

Determined to get better, really better, I decided I would return to see my naturopathic physician. She told me that I needed to get off the medication, and begin a program to help me completely regain my health. She ran many tests on me, and noted that one of the tests showed that my brain was low on lithium. That could be related to anxiety, and she advised me to detox from any heavy metals because they could contribute to anxiety. My blood pressure was also very low, which I found incredible. My blood pressure has never been low, so I just assumed her machine was broken. Of course, now that I think back on it, it would make sense that it was low considering I was taking the medications, but at the time, I just dismissed it—and dismissed her concerns about the lithium levels which really didn't mean much to me at the time. So I just went home and told Rick that I was going to start a whole new program and get off the allopathic medications for good and get back to being healthy.

I felt hopeful for the first time in ages. Calmed by the medication, I could think straight, and inspired by my naturopath, I knew I could stop the medication and get my health—and sanity—back. Little did I know, when I fell asleep that night, that the anaconda had recoiled—and by morning it would strike.

Waiting in Blood

Distress is an expression of the wisdom of
the body … it's a sign our somatic practice
is beginning to succeed … the body is
communicating information that needed
to come to our awareness.

REGINALD RAY

I HAVE LITTLE memory of the events that led up to that day. Later, Rick would tell me all about it, about how restless I'd been while sleeping, waking him early in the morning with my heavy breathing and panting, tossing and turning in what he thought was another one of my many nightmares. He knew something was very wrong, wrong enough that he even shook me awake, asked me questions to be sure I was oriented and aware of my surroundings.

"Judith, are you okay?" he asked me, thinking at first I was just tormented by my wild dreams.

My mumbled reply assured him that I was.

He noticed that my breathing was very irregular, kind of like twitches, and he thought it must be my medicine making me twitch. Nothing frightening, just weird. There had been so many restless nights and panicky days, that at first, it just seemed like another one. I remember getting up to pee, and suddenly feeling a sharp pain in the back of my head, as if someone had thrust an ice pick into my brain. This is no headache, I thought, as the excruciating pain at the back of my head brought me to my knees. I grabbed hold of the wall as I sunk to the floor, surrendering. The last thing I recall is calling to Rick for help.

—

"Rick, help me, something's wrong, hurry!" I remember calling out to Rick as I slumped to the floor, feeling the cold white linoleum as I lay crumpled and motionless. By the time Rick reached me, I was in agonizing pain. I don't remember anything after that.

Rick tells me that he took me into the living room, and helped me onto the couch. Suddenly I raced back to the bathroom and started throwing up. That's when he realized something was terribly wrong. He took me back to bed and checked my pupils to be sure they weren't dilated. He had been trained as an emergency medical technician when he was on ski patrol, so he immediately assessed the situation. He checked my eyes, and saw that they were red, but focused. Then he asked me to move my fingers and toes. I apparently did, but he still realized something was very, very wrong; he just didn't know what it was.

I was having a seizure, but Rick couldn't possibly have realized it at the time. I wasn't biting my tongue; I was barely responding to commands. My brain was in a world of its own; it had been damaged in the night, but on the outside, I just appeared to be having night terrors, dreamtime terrors that were tormenting me. At the same time, Rick was facing a waking nightmare of his very own as he struggled desperately to get a lucid response from me.

"Judith, Judith, can you hear me?" Rick's voice finally reached my consciousness—or so it seemed—and I began to respond. I still have no memory of those hours, but we have discussed them so many times since then that I feel as if his memories are my very own.

"I just feel really weird," I answered.

"What do you mean you feel weird?"

He was very worried because I was really spaced out, barely making any sense at all, as if I were there, but not there, like I was coming out of a very weird dream but still halfway in it.

By around 7 a.m., a good hour and a half later, I was still in that crazy state of oblivion, and he knew he had to do something. He called our nurse practitioner and she assured him it was not a response to the medication and that he should call a doctor. When he called our physician, he told Rick to bring me in right away so he could examine me. So after a bit of a battle to get me dressed—without much cooperation on my part—he put me into the car and drove me to the doctor's office. He took one look at me and noticed that I had blood in the retina of my eyes, known as Terson's Syndrome, which concerned him. Then he checked my neurological reflexes and noted that the Babinski Reflex in one foot was present which is not a good sign for an adult. It may indicate damage to the central nervous system.

"I don't know what it is; it could be spinal meningitis or a tumor," he told Rick, "but that wouldn't explain the blood in her eyes. We'd better get her in for an MRI right away."

I was apparently conscious through all this, but I have no memory of the visit. Everything I know about it I learned from Rick, and my medical records. Apparently I told them that the back of my head hurt a little bit, but other than that I was in no pain. I was clearly disoriented, though, and Rick knew that *something* was going on, something very wrong, so he took me for the MRI.

After the MRI, the technician told Rick the findings were negative, which is to say, there was nothing wrong with my brain. But Rick knew otherwise; he had seen me in all kinds of nervous states, he had seen me have panic attacks that were so severe I acted like a madwoman, and he had seen me drugged and disoriented from the tranquilizers. He *knew* that whatever was going on with me, it was something entirely different than anything I'd suffered before. And he knew that I had been taking medication, and that medications have side effects. He wasn't about to take me home until he was certain I was okay.

Instead, we left and were admitted through the Emergency Room at the University of Washington Hospital for observation and more tests, and that's where I stayed for the next eight hours, so disoriented that I still don't recall those long hours.

"We'll need to do some more tests and order a CT scan," a doctor told Rick, "but from what I can tell from the MRI, there have been some changes in her brain."

"*Changes in her brain?*" Rick was stunned. Why had he been told the MRI was negative if there were changes in my brain? Why hadn't *anyone* noticed that much earlier? Worse, Rick thought, why hadn't he realized himself how serious it was earlier in the morning, when I first woke up, and called 911 instead of other people? Of course, Rick had no way of knowing how serious it was when I first woke up, and given how many nightmares I'd had in the past, naturally he'd assumed it was just another one.

Hearing the news that something had happened to my brain really shook Rick, and he began to second guess himself. In fact, he *had* acted quickly—I had never lost consciousness, but he knew something was wrong, he had checked my vital signs, he had called several people for advice—and instead of waiting to see what happened as so many people advised, Rick called a doctor. And he rushed me to that doctor, and followed his advice and rushed me to the hospital. If it weren't for Rick's presence, I have no doubt I would have died that day. He saved my life, but at that point in time he was so afraid that I *would* die that he was berating himself with worry and guilt about what he could have done differently. What he could have done differently was wait it out to see what happened—if he had done *that*, I hate to think what would have happened! I will be forever grateful that Rick acted so quickly and diligently to find out what was wrong with me and get me the treatment that I needed even as I fought him and resisted getting dressed and going anywhere.

I barely remember the ride to the hospital. My conscious mind returned briefly as we drove by the university as I was talking on the phone to my close friend Lisa. I remember being very frightened, and her assuring me that everything would be fine. Later she would tell me that she didn't believe it herself, but kept repeating words of comfort for me and for herself.

But I don't remember reaching the hospital or much of anything that first day. Apparently, I appeared to be aware of what was going on. Rick told me that when we got there, they started asking me questions to see how aware I was, and when they asked me who the president was, I asked if I really had to say his name. "George Bush," I finally told them, wincing, and the doctor was reassured that I had at least retained some awareness of the outside world even if I didn't agree with its politics.

I answered all their other questions with sufficient awareness so that they were the ones who were confused. They were having a hard time figuring out what was wrong with me—the MRI had shown nothing unusual in my brain. So they decided to do more tests. Then I suddenly began throwing up blood, and they knew something serious was going on, so they pumped my stomach. When they found nothing in my stomach, they ordered a lumbar puncture or spinal tap to look at my Cerebral Spinal Fluid.

Meanwhile, Rick was becoming genuinely terrified. The more he sought answers, the more confused everyone just seemed to be, but he knew one thing—something had happened to my brain in the night and as far as he could tell from my disorientation and vomiting blood, whatever it was, it was still happening. So he called a friend of ours, Karen, a CST practitioner I'd known for years, and asked her to come to the hospital.

Karen hurried over and gave Rick a break, and when he returned he found me sitting up in bed shortly, as lucid as ever.

"Hi Rick!" I said in a cheery tone, as if he'd stumbled upon me at a festive party, rather than sitting in a hospital bed hooked up to a lace-work of IV's, as I was. Rick was utterly stunned to see me in such spirits. When he'd left me, I was barely aware that he was even there, and when he returned, I looked to be healthier than I'd been in years.

"Judith!" he said, stumbling over his words in obvious shock, "what happened? You're all better!"

"They don't know what's going on," I told him, now fully aware of everything that was happening, "but I feel great! My head hurts a little bit, but they gave me some pain meds so I'm feeling no pain!"

We chatted away for awhile, Rick, Karen and I, laughing and joking about my crazy brain, when the doctor arrived for the lumbar puncture—that would tell him whether or not there was any blood in my Cerebral Spinal Fluid—which would probably mean that an artery had ruptured. I began thrashing and Karen and Rick had to help hold me down while the doctor inserted the long needle into the base of my spine. Karen—as she would later tell me—knew right away that something was wrong because the fluid that flowed into the syringe was pink—a sure sign that there was a bleed somewhere; unless it was from the puncture itself.

The hospital staff asked Karen to leave the room for a few minutes while they conferred with Rick, and when she returned, she said that I looked at her like she was a nurse and cheerfully said, "Hi, you look just like my good friend, Karen!"

She replied, "I *am* Karen, Judith!" and she knew then that I was okay, and that I had not suffered any major brain damage from the bleed because I was alert and could recognize her. A bit disoriented, to be sure—after all, I was oblivious to the fact that she'd just been in my room talking with me.

Then a doctor came in and gave us some news.

"We found blood in your Cerebral Spinal Fluid," he said somberly, immediately smothering the cheer in the room. Of course, Karen had noticed this, but she hadn't said anything to me or Rick, knowing it would only upset us and the doctors would let us know soon enough.

Blood in my CSF? That didn't sound good, not at all good. But before either Rick or I could mutter much more than a perplexed "Huh?" the doctor continued.

"Because of the puncture, the pressure on her brain has subsided, which is why she's coherent. She has an artery rupture somewhere in her brain; we just don't know the exact location yet."

I was scared and very confused, but before I could say anything, Rick interjected.

"Let's run a CT scan right away," Rick said, authoritatively. After all, the doctors had been saying they'd run a CT scan ever since we arrived.

The doctor told the nurses to prep me for a CT scan. As time went on, I became increasingly disoriented. When they asked me again what year it was, instead of answering 2008, which it was, I said it was 1953, 1955, all sorts of years a half century before. They knew that whatever it was, it was progressing, and they hurried me downstairs for the CT scan.

By the time it was over it was growing dark outside. I would be spending the night in the hospital. My body and brain had suffered an incredible trauma, and between the trauma and the medication they'd given me, I just drifted in and out of sleep.

Then the doctor returned.

"I'm afraid the results were positive," he told Rick. Somehow being told the tests were "positive" was only more confusing. After all, positive usually means something good, but in this case, we knew it was bad. The doctor explained, "We found the aneurysm and where it has ruptured."

"An aneurysm!?" Rick asked, having hoped the tests would rule out anything so serious, but now feeling as if he'd just heard the worst possible news they could deliver. "You mean Judith's had a stroke?"

"It's a matter of terminology. An aneurysm is a swelling of an artery. A stroke is the leaking or rupture of the artery. An aneurysm is literally a bulging of the arterial wall, as if the artery had ballooned out. It doesn't always rupture and in fact she probably had the aneurysm a long time. Her brain is still getting blood flow, of course, which is why she's able to communicate at all, but the aneurysm caused the arterial wall to bulge, forming a blood-filled sac which burst. That's why she had a seizure. Now we're facing a brain hemorrhage."

"What does that mean?" Rick asked nervously, "Will she be okay? How can we stop it? Will she need surgery?"

"She'll be stable for the rest of the night," the doctor told him, "but in the morning we need to transfer her to Harborview. They're the leading trauma center in the Pacific Northwest, and she'll be treated by some of the country's best specialists in aneurysms there. They'll advise you on the best course of treatment."

In other words, my brain was damaged, or nearly damaged.

The following morning I was transferred to and prepped for surgery. Finally, Rick was advised that although the typical procedure for treating a brain aneurysm was cutting into the skull and snipping off the broken section of artery, there was a less invasive treatment that might work. It is called the Coil Method. They would repair the rupture with a coil of titanium. They would insert a thin plastic catheter into my femoral artery beginning at my groin area, snake their way up through my vascular system to the base of my brain and leave a tightly knotted coil of titanium fibers in the swollen arterial sac that lay at the base of my brain. By weaving the sac with knotted titanium, there would be no repeated rupture—and instead, my blood would—hopefully—flow normally again, slightly re-routed. If that didn't work, they told Rick, they would cut open my skull.

"We really don't know what we're going to find, until we get started," a neurosurgeon told him, "but we have to tell you if we have to cut into her skull, there could be damage. Hopefully the less invasive Coil Method will work." Hopefully. Rick was barely holding on, doing his best to appear calm and strong and make good decisions, all the while being told that my brain had nearly burst in the night and I would need a form of brain surgery.

When they began talking about medical directives, he realized for the first time that I might really die. I had learned much from working with many brain-damaged clients, so I'd long ago written a medical directive instructing Rick not to do anything to prolong my life in the event of brain death. At the time it had always seemed like a practical document that every adult should have on hand. There was no emotional impact in signing it, nor in discussing it. But now that the doctors were asking him to produce it, and wanting him to sign it as well, Rick nearly fell to pieces. The very real possibility that at any moment I might be brain dead suddenly overwhelmed him. He called our doctor, who kept a copy of the directive in my file, and consulted with him. Our doctor advised, "You have to give her a chance by going through with the surgery. We'll deal with the prolonging life issue afterward." Rick felt reassured by his words, and knew he had no choice but to agree to the surgery.

"Go home and get some sleep," the neurosurgeon told him, "she's going to be out for the night and you really need to rest. You can sign these in the morning."

By about two in the morning, Rick left, still stunned, but feeling better just knowing he didn't have to sign the directive that night.

The next morning when he returned, however, the issue of signing the medical directive was raised once again.

"What happens if she doesn't have the surgery?" Rick asked.

"She'll be dead by tomorrow," they told him. He was stunned, feeling as if I had died already.

"Before I sign anything," he asked the team of neurosurgeons, "just how many of these things you have done? I'm not sure I want Judith being a guinea pig for any experimental surgery."

"Oh, we've done about twenty thousand, give or take a thousand," a doctor said reassuringly, and another added, "it's a very common procedure; it isn't experimental. There have been dozens of studies over the last decade that have shown that the Coil Method is safe and effective for the right patient. It really only works on a minority of patients, I'm afraid, and we have to decide on the best method of treatment on a case by case method. Although the Coil Method doesn't work for everyone, I want to give it a try before doing anything more invasive. If it turns out that we have to consider more invasive surgery, then that's what we'll do. We won't know until we get in there with the fluoroscope and see exactly where it is in relation to other arteries."

That explanation eased Rick's worries considerably, though not entirely, and he signed the papers, all the while fearing the very real possibility that I might not survive the procedure. For all their talk of how safe it was, they sure did want him to sign a lot of papers acknowledging he understood all the terrible things that could happen! These terrible things they called "risks" included death, dementia and paralysis just to name a few. What could happen if I did not have the surgery was more certain, and Rick knew that the coil procedure was our best and safest bet for my recovery at that point.

Meanwhile, as all this was going on I was being shuffled back and forth for more tests, more CT scans, and more prep. The blood in my eyes hadn't subsided at all, and if anything had gotten worse. During the aneurysm, it seems, blood had flowed along my optic nerve to the retinas of my eyes. My eyes hurt all the time and I kept them closed as much as possible. Everything I saw was through a curtain of red, and the doctors said if it didn't clear up by itself I would have to have surgery on my eyes. The idea of eye surgery really frightened me, but I tried to keep my spirits up. I was apparently coherent, talking with Rick and the doctors and telling them how everything I saw was like looking through rose-colored glasses, but they were focused on a much more serious procedure—tying a knot of titanium in my brain.

As they prepped me for the procedure, a nurse explained everything to Rick, telling him what they were doing and why, and that calmed him a lot. When they wheeled me into the operating room, the nurse again explained what they'd be doing to me while I was in there, and told Rick it would be from two to five hours before he'd see me again.

Those hours were torture for Rick, who didn't know if I would live or die. When he called his friend Karl, a school teacher, to tell him what was going on, Karl immediately called his school and told them he had an emergency and could not go to work that day, and he rushed to the hospital. I don't know what Rick would have done without Karl; just having his friend by his side helped him to get through those long and agonizing hours of waiting for me to come out of surgery.

After I was wheeled into surgery, Rick and Karl went downstairs to the cafeteria to get something to eat when Karl took one look at the food sitting under the heat lamps and said, "Let's get the hell out of here."

Rick didn't want to leave me and protested, but Karl persisted. "There's nothing we can do here but wait. We can sit here and be nervous or we can go outside for a walk."

That was exactly what Rick needed, so they walked around the neighborhood and had some lunch, and then wandered over to another restaurant where they drank some tequila. After a couple of shots of tequila

Rick finally began to calm down when his cell phone rang. It was the hospital calling, and for a moment, Rick froze. He couldn't wait to hear the news, but if it was bad, he knew he'd fall apart. When he answered it, the voice on the other end told him that everything went well and I was recovering in ICU. Rick and Karl let out a cheer and raced out of the restaurant and hiked back to the hospital in much higher spirits—literally and figuratively -- than when they'd left.

Meanwhile, when I came out of surgery, the nurses who were hovering over me told me I'd had brain surgery and the doctors had put a "coil" in my brain. I was still so out of it that I had no memory of anything since feeling the ice pick sensation in my head. *Brain surgery? A coil in my head?* What did either of those concepts mean? I struggled for a moment to understand what they were telling me, to orient myself to the strange surroundings. Then I wiggled my fingers and toes and whooped for joy! I wasn't paralyzed! I scanned my interior knowledge of my body. My eyes worked, although they really hurt and everything was reddish. I was talking, laughing, sensing—I didn't seem to have any problems with my brain. They said something about an aneurysm, and I thought that meant a stroke. Had I had a stroke? I touched my face, and it seemed evenly aligned, nothing was drooping or drooling. What did brain surgery mean? Did they cut open my head? I felt my head and my hair. My hair was all there—how could I have had brain surgery if they hadn't shaved my hair? I was so confused, but as I felt my head, it was familiar territory. As a professional CranioSacral therapist, the head was my expertise. Nothing seemed off, my head was intact, aligned, no bandages, scars, missing patches of hair.

I began to scan my body's interior, doing the body-sensing work in which I was so well trained. I sensed nothing unusual; but I *was* in a hospital and I was seeing everything through a veil of red. My eyes hurt so badly …hmm, something was wrong, even if I couldn't feel it in my drugged body, waking up in the ICU with nurses telling me I'd just had brain surgery and a coil put into my brain was definitely not normal. What was that about a coil in my brain? And where was Rick?

Rick was racing back to me, and by the time Rick got to the ICU, his nerves were spiking again—everyone he passed was on some sort of ventilator, looking as if they'd reached the ends of their lives. All he could think of was that if I didn't die, I could be a vegetable or paralyzed or unable to communicate. He couldn't imagine how damaged I would be, and every possible horrible outcome went through his head as he searched for me amidst all the beds of patients recovering from surgery. Then he saw me.

"Hi!" I said, greeting Rick. Instead of finding me half-comatose and breathing through a hose, he found me chatting on the phone to a friend, telling her "I just had *brain* surgery!" I was whooping and hollering with exhilaration. Rick was absolutely astounded—he had been expecting any possible horror, but he sure wasn't prepared for me to be so happy! Then he realized, of course, that I was totally stoned on the powerful narcotics they'd given me! Once he saw that I wasn't paralyzed, he was ecstatic.

I wiggled my fingers and I wiggled my toes to show him that everything worked! "Yahoo!" I yelled like a giddy cowgirl riding a wild bronco while Rick looked on in amazement. "All my parts are working!"

Except of course, my eyes. I was still seeing red, and as thrilled as I was that everything else seemed to be in working order, I wondered if I might spend the rest of my life looking at the world through lenses of red blood. Or was all that red a sign of something else going on? I felt fine, I felt thrilled to be alive, but I also felt afraid. Something had happened to my brain, and I wasn't out of the woods yet.

"We won't know for a few days," the doctors told me, "the extent of the damage . . ." Their words were lost to me. I was in a narcotic-fueled cloud and wouldn't remember much in the days and weeks to come.

Chocolate Cake,
Salt & Laughter

The brain needs stimulation from the
body…the body is organized to recover,
so if you help the circulation to normalize,
and recover the sensitivity by
stimulating the skin, (it) begins
to recover in its own way.

GERDA ALEXANDER

FOR THE NEXT two weeks, Rick practically lived at the hospital, coming early in the morning and staying late into the night. I wasn't left alone, however. Girlfriends slept in the Lazy-Boy chair next to my bed, and watched me almost constantly, while other friends came and went. My mother flew in, along with my sister, Susan, and I was pampered like a movie star—although I was not conscious of all the attention!

Rick brought me the Green and White Tara paintings from home to make my corner of the ICU feel more intimate and personal. "The Taras," as I refer to them, are Buddhist images of female deities; Green Tara represents protection, and White Tara represents healing, serenity and long life—which is exactly what I needed. We had only recently acquired the Taras, almost as if we had intuitively sensed their need, and having them placed by the bed in my room helped me to feel centered and protected.

Rick was also concerned about the quality of food they were serving in the hospital. He brought me healthy food from the local co-op and he even went downstairs to the cafeteria, where food was served to the public, and asked to see a menu for the coming week. He began ordering off that menu—which offered far better food than the standard fare they brought to patients. I had no appetite for quite some time, no matter how good the food might have been, and pretty much stuck to a diet of applesauce and pills. I was still in critical condition and not out of danger by any means.

The doctors explained to Rick and my family that they feared my brain might start hemorrhaging, and noted that I was already having small spasms in my brain. Spasms could shut off blood flow, and cause another stroke, so they did an ultrasound to monitor their frequency.

I was hooked up to so many tubes and hoses that I looked like the backside of a home entertainment center, nothing but cables and cords. I'd had so many needles inserted into me that my arms were all shot and my veins had collapsed and they feared I'd get an infection. So they put in what they called a "trunk line"—a portal that was inserted into my right shoulder area which could then be hooked up to any drug or fluid they needed to pump into me. First in line was the morphine.

I could pump the morphine drip as needed, whenever the pain in my body got to be too much to bear as I recovered. Apparently I really liked the morphine and pumped it quite a lot! But Rick was wary of giving me too much and he knew I had enough medicines in my body at the time—they had me on blood thinners, stool softeners, chemical balancers and every other possible chemical that would keep my body functioning. Despite my happy trigger finger on the morphine pump, Rick knew that I did not like pharmaceutical medicines at all. He had always teased me about my reliance on herbs, telling me that herbs were just as powerful as pharmaceutical medicines; I'd put any herb into my body, but resist taking any pharmaceutical medicines that might make me better. He always reminded me, too, that just because a medicine was an herb it didn't mean it wasn't toxic. Over the years, I'd persisted in relying on herbal and homeopathic medicines while rejecting allopathic pharmaceutical medicines. Now, however, pharmaceutical medicines were keeping me alive, and keeping the pain at bay.

While I was supposed to be resting during this period, it seemed as if my "room"—the curtained off ICU cubicle that enclosed my bed—was incredibly busy. The phlebotomists were stopping by every few hours for blood work, even at night. Every few hours I would be woken up so the nurses could take my blood pressure and ask me "those" neuro-logical assessment questions about the president and all to see if I was still aware. It was exhausting and all I wanted was to just sleep without interruption, but I had a severe brain injury, and they couldn't afford to allow me that luxury. My body had to be constantly monitored or I could have another unrecognized stroke or cerebral hemorrhage, or a heart attack at any moment.

The ophthalmology team dropped by once a day to assess my eyes— which were still filled with blood, making their faces appear dark pink— and they shined lights into my eyes and clucked and whispered over my head like a flock of flustered chickens. I was so drowsy I didn't always follow their chatter, but when I heard them talking about possible future surgeries, I cringed and crossed my index fingers, forming a hex sign in front of my heart to ward them off. There'd be no more surgeries for me! One brain aneurysm was enough!

The neurologists stopped by my bed twice a day. They came in large groups since it was a teaching hospital: my brain had become a case for them to study! The nurses would always tip me off right before they arrived, so I would sit up and primp my hair and pretend I was feeling much better—and even if I didn't *feel* better, as far as I was concerned as long as I wasn't dead I *was* better. Whenever they came I would bow to thank them for their good work, holding my palms together, grateful to be blessed with my life.

This was my life at Harborview Medical Center, the award-winning trauma center in the Pacific Northwest. I couldn't even see the view of the harbor very well because my sore eyes were painful and blood soaked. All I saw was a plain red hospital world when my sore and dusty eyes were opened, which wasn't very often. The blood from the cerebral aneurysm had traveled down both optic nerves like the time the rain seeped into my home when the skylight leaked, trickling along an electrical wire, leaving a pool of water on the closet floor. My eyes were like that closet, the blood pooling inside them, making it so difficult to see the world.

But I could hear. I could hear the constant thump-thump-thump of the helicopters landing on the roof of the hospital, bringing in the severely wounded whose lives depended on every second saved. Day in, day out, the helicopters landed, so noisy and so close. Their noise woke me throughout the day, and with each landing reminded me that yet another life was hovering between tragedy and triumph. My own life was fast becoming one of triumph, I realized. I was so grateful to peer through the veil of blood and see my friends and family, to know that I would be okay. I was going to be okay . . .

Still, I knew I was far from out of the woods. The doctors told Rick that I had an irregular heart beat and they had to keep an eye on that, in case I had a heart attack on top of everything else.

"In any post-traumatic brain injury," a doctor told Rick, "we're looking at one of two scenarios, cerebral salt wasting or salt retention. Either the patient will excrete all of their salt, or they will retain it all. In either case, we have to closely monitor the electrolytes and be sure she stays hydrated."

"Cerebral salt wasting?" Rick asked, "I've never heard of that. What does that mean?"

"It means her blood isn't retaining salt. But I wouldn't worry about that, it's relatively rare."

"But if it happens? What would happen to Judith?"

"She'll self medicate for starters."

"Self medicate? You mean the morphine pump?"

"No, nothing like that. She'll start by craving salt. She'll eat as much salt as she can possibly get. It's not uncommon for patients to crave things like pickle juice, which has a high sodium content. It's nothing we want to mess around with. It leads to serious dehydration, and can cause dangerously low blood pressure, irregular heartbeat, anxiety, panic, a number of things."

"But she already has an irregular heartbeat," Rick pointed out, worried that I might have 'cerebral salt wasting.'

"Yes, which is why we want to be sure it doesn't worsen. Don't worry; we'll keep a close eye on the sodium levels in her blood. But as I've said, it's relatively rare, though we do see it now and again in post-traumatic brain injuries."

Rick was relieved to hear that cerebral salt wasting was rare, but worried in case I got it. And sure enough, within a week, just as I was getting much, much better, my sodium levels dropped dramatically and I got much, much worse. Where I'd been very coherent, eating well and feeling great, I suddenly went downhill. I was barely coherent, and no matter how much oxygen they gave me, I couldn't get enough. They had me hooked up to an oxygen tank and were giving me the maximum level, but I felt as if I were suffocating. I was really laboring just to breathe, and my heart rate shot up so dramatically that my heart was racing, while my mind was just drifting in and out of awareness. I was so groggy and couldn't stay awake, I just slept and slept and slept. They gave me these giant salt tablets that I would swallow with applesauce; Rick later told me that I ate half a dozen in less than four hours, and still wanted more! They could have hung a giant salt lick over my bed and I probably would have sucked every last crystal just to get more salt in my body.

Rick was expecting me to be really sick when I came out of surgery, and thrilled when I was so alert and doing fine. To see me suddenly plummet like that and become so disoriented was re-traumatizing for him—it was as if Rick was going through the aneurysm all over again and it left him very nervous to realize even if I looked like I was fine I could become seriously sick again at any moment. My metabolism just would not stabilize. My condition worsened for several days, with the nurses staying by my bedside round the clock, while Rick, again, was terrified he would lose me.

The stress on Rick was so great that even though he tried to eat, he was losing weight fast. Eventually, our friends and family realized that while the nurses were keeping an eye on me, someone needed to help Rick. One day, it happened to be his friend William's birthday. Rick was glad to see him and his family when they dropped by for a visit on their way to a celebratory dinner.

"You need to get out of here," William told him, "You need to get your mind off this for awhile. Judith will be okay, the nurses will keep an eye on her, and her sister is here."

"No, I can't leave," Rick told him, "Judith's gotten really bad." Even though everyone tried to reassure him that I'd be okay, Rick was really freaked out about leaving me even for a minute.

"Come on, man," William said firmly, "You're leaving this place and you're going to help me celebrate my birthday."

Rick was far too worried to consider celebrating anything, and insisted he couldn't go anywhere and had to stay with me. My sister knew that if he didn't have a change of focus he would just become more stressed, and we needed him to be strong.

"Nope, Rick," she told him, "You are going to dinner with them. Now go on downstairs!" Her assertiveness was just what Rick needed at that moment, and he knew that my sister was making a decision that was for my benefit, so he let her take the lead.

"Okay, then, I guess I'm out of here," he told them. He tried telling me he was leaving but I was just too out of it to make much sense at all. About all he got out of me was "Okay, fine, whatever," and then I was once again lost to the oblivion of morphine and illness.

So the group had dinner and celebrated William's birthday, and Rick began to feel better. He was still worried sick, of course, but disconnecting from the hospital environment was truly just what he needed to help him to focus and regain his clarity.

When William's wife suggested they bring me something from the restaurant, Rick didn't think that was such a good idea. He told her I hadn't wanted to eat anything at all, I was so out of it.

"This is the worst I've seen her," he said, trying to convince her that getting birthday cake "to go" was a bad idea, "She's been going downhill for the last two days and I don't think she's in any shape for cake."

"Well we'll see," William's wife said, optimistically. "This *is* an awesome chocolate cake."

They brought Rick back to the hospital and he came to my room with the birthday cake, expecting to set it on the bedside table and hold my hand while I withered away.

Instead, he saw me sitting up with a smile!

"Hi, Rick!" I said, as cheerful as ever, "How are you? I feel great!"

Rick stood there, practically paralyzed with shock, when William said, "Here Judith, we brought you something!"

"Ohhhh . . ." I said, as excited as a little girl, "What's this?" I reached out my hands for the paper bag they were holding.

"We brought you a piece of this awesome chocolate cake!" their son said.

"Oh, wow, hand it over!" I said, ready to dig in.

Rick handed me the take-out bag and I tore into it like a ravenous tiger, devouring it so fast that he just stood there in utter bewilderment. He was prepared to see me lying half-dead in a coma, but he sure wasn't prepared to see me gobbling up chocolate cake and babbling away as if nothing had happened.

"Wait a minute!" he said, trying to wrap his head around this sudden shift from nearly dead to wide awake and starving. "Two hours ago you were almost dead! You haven't eaten a thing for two days and now you're eating *chocolate cake*? Well, I guess that just goes to show what happens when you finally get your electrolytes balanced!"

We laughed and jabbered like kids at a slumber party and for the first time, I was fully present. Remember, I really have little or no memory of any of these events up to this time, with the exception of the ride to the hospital, and have had to have Rick and my friends fill me in on what was really had happened. But some memories do remain, though the details are fuzzy. For example, besides the chocolate cake, I remember this really rowdy guy in a cubicle next to mine—it seemed that all he wanted to do was smoke and watch videos! Plus my bed was really uncomfortable—it felt so hard and lumpy. I remember feeling so exhausted but so restless, trying to find a comfortable position. And I remember gazing at the ugliest orange striped curtains I'd ever seen.

I especially remember that the ICU nurses were absolutely fantastic. They were so efficient, skilled and compassionate and did everything possible to comfort me. We chatted a lot, because they thought it was so ironic that I was a CranioSacral therapist and who had a brain aneurysm. I could talk about anatomy in medical terms and we could discuss what they were doing. I understood what was happening to my body in a clinical and sensory manner which they found really interesting. It seemed that I was explaining as much to them about what was happening to my body as they were explaining to me!

Once the salt wasting had been stabilized, it was as if I had finally reclaimed my brain—but I was to find that truly reclaiming my brain would take some more time, but at least I was at last waking up.

As I began to recover, my appetite came back and I was enjoying more of what Rick ordered for me. He had really figured out how to order good meals for me at the hospital. One evening, when he was at a meeting, I ordered by myself and looked forward all afternoon to a delicious chicken dinner. But when it came, I lifted off the stainless steel cover to see a lonely naked piece of pale boiled chicken sitting in the center of an empty white plate. So unappetizing! I was crestfallen. Rick knew the secrets of ordering and eating well at that hospital!

Just then, happily, our friends Robin and Max showed up to rescue me.

"Let's get you something better," Robin suggested, and she and Max went down to the cafeteria and returned with some tofu and green beans, thinking that would suit me. My eyes were closed when they got back and I smelled this wonderful aroma of something really delicious.

"No, I want whatever smells so good!" I said, opening my eyes and seeing that Max had brought back a hamburger for himself and was about to bite into it. He offered it to me, I reached over, and took a huge bite. Then right before their eyes I ate every last bite as if I hadn't been fed in days. Come to think of it, I *hadn't* eaten in days! I'd had so little food while they were trying to balance my electrolytes from the salt wasting that I was utterly famished and any food that entered my room was going straight into my mouth! With my appetite returning I realized that hunger—one of the survival mechanisms of humans—was kicking in. I was getting better!

One day a nurse came into my room and said, "Okay, now, we're going downstairs for an MRI." He had a gurney but I wondered if I could walk by myself instead. Up to this point I had been confined to a bed. I would find out what it felt like to walk.

I looked up to the man and with a feeble smile said, "Sure…" although I was totally *unsure* of whether or not I could make it. I moved myself out of bed and tentatively took a few steps—I could walk! What an incredible joy! I held onto the gurney and followed the metal moving bed to the elevator. I felt my bare feet on the cool floor. My hips and legs were moving normally. My balance needed a lot of attention, but I felt my brain reorganizing myself into a standing and walking mode. I soon walked comfortably down the hall to the elevator. Descending in the elevator was another weird sensation to adjust to; my brain was at school today!

We arrived in the MRI dungeon. It was very still—we probably weren't far from the morgue. All the bustling hospital energy was gone. It felt eerie, to be surrounded by such silence. And then I saw the machine. It looked so frightening, like a space-aged coffin. The thought of lying down in that steel tube made me freeze as if I were paralyzed.

"Do I have to go in?" I asked the technician.

"Why not?" he replied, cheerfully. "You've been in this baby several times already!"

I had no memory of ever having been in it before! I did as he said, I got on the table and remained motionless, barely breathing. It seemed to take forever. My thoughts began to wander as I imagined my DNA spinning in a strange magnetic field. I had heard about these machines from my clients and from Dr. Upledger. The loud dissonant cacophony hurt my ears. The chaotic overstimulation swept through my brain like a tornado. I focussed on my breath so I didn't get swept up in it. Finally it was over! Later, back in my room, I was told that my arteries looked great!

—

Soon, holding onto my IV cart, I began walking up and down the corridors, walking to the windows to look out at the distant water, enjoying the artwork by the elevators. When I peeked into some of the other rooms as I passed by, I was shocked to see so many people on ventilators and in various uncomfortable positions because of the severity of their strokes. I had to keep reminding myself that I was in the neuropsych ward where only the most serious cases were sent. Although I felt much improved, I had, after all, had brain surgery.

—

I'd been in the ICU for twelve days—nearly two weeks of twenty-four hour intensive care—before I was moved upstairs to the critical care unit where there were fewer nurses. It felt much more like a "self serve" unit compared to ICU, and Rick became more involved in my care. He helped me to get in and out of bed, to go to the bathroom, help me eat, find nurses when I needed them—he did practically *everything* to nurture me back to health.

Getting me into the shower however, seemed to be more than he wanted to handle. I so desperately wanted a real shower, but the nurses were always so busy that the most they had time for were sponge baths. The new room had a large walk-in shower. I was still too unstable to shower by myself, even with handrails, so when a friend, Carolyn, who was studying to be a naturopathic physician, came by, she gave Rick a break and helped me take a shower; she just went right into the shower with me!

The whole time I was in the hospital many friends dropped by and helped me with a lot of hands-on body work and energy work. They brought me food, talked with me and read to me. My eyes still felt dry and very painful, so I continued to keep them closed a lot, but I knew that they worked and were getting better. The blood-soaked veil through which I saw the world had turned to brownish-red speckles that Rick jokingly called my "dead pixels."

The medications were rapidly being excreted from my body and I was feeling more energetic by the hour. Once I could start showering and eating well, I wanted to get home to my own bed. After three or four more days, the doctors said they felt I had recovered sufficiently to go home. Assured that Rick—who was working from home at the time—would be with me, they discharged me a day early with instructions to come straight back to the hospital's emergency ward if I felt any pain in my head.

When you try to get *into* a hospital it can take forever just to get admitted and get a bed, unless you arrive in an ambulance from another hospital as I did. But when they want you *out,* it happens very quickly. As soon as they told me I was being discharged, there was a whirlwind of activity to get me out of there. We'd been there for two weeks and had a lot of stuff laying around but they were practically rushing us out the door once they decided I'd be okay. It felt very hectic as we waited to get the medications I would need and to pack up our belongings. I found the whole experience very startling as I realized I was being hurried out the door to make room for the next patient.

The drive home felt like a dream because it was such a beautiful fall day. However, I was shaken by the abrupt departure and the realization that everything I saw was still bathed in red—and might be for the rest of my life –and I began to wonder if I was really ready to return home. I hadn't even seen my surgeon before I left; instead I was told to come back to see him in a few weeks.

How exactly would my body heal? What would I do when Rick was at a meeting or out on an errand? We had an on-call nurse we could contact if there were an emergency, but no other help and the thought of being alone at home for even a few minutes really scared me. The drive itself felt frightening—after being immobilized for so long, I was suddenly in a car with my dear husband driving me home and it felt like we were moving too fast. Going from zero to sixty miles an hour was startling; it reminded me of driving out of the mountains after a week of walking with a heavy backpack strapped to my back on wilderness trails. Everything suddenly seemed to be going by at the speed of light.

—

We soon arrived home. It was a classically beautiful October with warm sun, squash-colored maple leaves and a crystal-clear Tibetan dark blue sky. I slept like a cat, waking momentarily only to move and follow the sun and return to sleep as soon as I could.

I knew I would recover and rarely thought about the brain injury at all, though I could tell it was very much on Rick's mind. He wanted me to take my time recovering so that my brain fully healed. But for some reason, ever since I woke up in the ICU, I had the intuitive sense that I would be fine. I'm not sure why, but I just knew that I would be okay. I was learning to trust my body's wisdom and the ways of the universe.

I began to take little walks in the neighborhood, and would invite my friends over to walk with me. At first the walks—maybe only five minutes long—soon grew longer. I was beginning to get my physical energy back but my brain would still tire very easily. I had no interest in music or the visual stimulation of movies to pass the time—that was too much for me to process. Even being read to for an hour was tiring. I needed quiet time, and my home became my retreat as I recovered. I loved just sitting, meditating on the autumn beauty and the joy of my renewal.

Eventually my walks became more brisk, and I was able to work with myself to help my healing by practicing yoga for stretching and strengthening my body and Qi Gong, an ancient Chinese technique of using the mind and movement to open energy meridians. The doctors hadn't recommended any physical therapy which was fine with me; I knew the most efficient therapies that would help me to recover. My friends in the bodywork community gave me tremendous support and helped me as I discharged trauma from the stomach pumping I'd had in the E.R.; gave me brain treatments for neurological tissue reorganization, Lymphatic Drainage, Visceral Manipulation, CranioSacral Therapy, and acupuncture—all methods of the bodywork I had studied and which I knew would help me. I also did Awareness Through Movement lessons to work directly with the motor and sensory neurons of the brain through a variety of movement sequences.

—

One evening, a week after I had been home, I was waiting for a visit from a friend and resting on the Feldenkrais table in our living room. It's a wide bench covered with dense foam and vinyl, and built in such a way that it gives the body and brain direct sensory feedback. I was lying there when I noticed my hands traveling up to my neck and occipital bone. I was just fiddling with the tissues that felt uncomfortable when I found a line of tension that went from the area of my brain where the coil had been placed toward my lower neck area. It wasn't anything I would call a headache, but I casually mentioned to Rick that I could feel some tension and he immediately went into action.

"Come on," he said, wasting no time, "We're taking you back to the hospital."

"Why?" I said, not wanting to go anywhere.

"Because that's what they told us to do," he answered firmly, "they said if your head starts hurting, we go to the E.R. So let's go."

"But my head *isn't* hurting," I protested, "I can just feel a fascial line of scar tissue or tension, that's all."

"Then you're in denial," he said, "I know you, and you are usually very aware of your body. It might just feel like a fascial tension to you, but you're feeling *something* wrong. We're going straight to the E.R."

I groaned at the thought. "I can't stand the thought of seeing those orange striped curtains one more time!" I wailed. But I knew that there was no sense arguing; he meant business. Just as we were getting into the car, my friend arrived and we told her what was going on. She agreed to join us and we all piled into the car and took off.

On arrival, because I still had my hospital identification bracelet on my wrist, they whisked me past all the street people and mothers with sobbing children—the sad testimonial to healthcare for our poor who get treated in the E.R. but not in a doctor's office. I felt ashamed to be ushered in so quickly when it was clear they had been waiting for hours. I wanted to shout that I had just had brain surgery so they wouldn't think I was just cutting the line because I wasn't poor.

Then I was shuffled around for all sorts of tests and scans and hours and hours of waiting. Finally a doctor came to our alcove sometime around three a.m. to say that they couldn't see anything wrong inside my head so it was probably just "healing pains." We were so exhausted we just laughed. It seemed so ludicrous because I knew what those "healing pains" were. I truly *was* feeling a line of tension along the artery where the coil instrument had travelled, a path I would get to know well in the coming years—for soon I would feel it down to the top of my thigh, past the insertion point in the femoral artery and down my leg, the lymph gathering and swelling as the tissues groaned and pulled from the invasion. They do call the coil procedure "invasive surgery" after all. So I realized that what I had been feeling was the scar tissue and the beginning of my healing process—"healing pains."

—

We'd arrived at the hospital in the evening but by the time we got out of there it was nearly dawn and I felt the whole adventure had been unnecessary. I didn't want to go through anything like that again just to be told I was fine and could go home, and I told Rick so. I said that was the last time I was rushing back to the hospital just because my head hurt. But he was adamant.

"Oh, no, if your head starts hurting again, we're going back again. I'm not making the same mistake twice!"

"What mistake?" I asked him, "They said I was fine!"

"I don't mean this time," he said, "I mean the first time. I never should have waited so long to take you in when you woke up so disoriented."

I realized then that Rick was still berating and judging himself for not doing more, even though he'd done everything right and had saved my life by taking me in when he did. The neurosurgeon had told us the outcome wouldn't have been any different if I'd gone in sooner, only if we had delayed a day or two. After all, the only real concern I had at this point was my vision, and the blood was slowly draining from my eyes and my vision was improving, though I still feared I might be permanently partially blind. I was just incredibly relieved I was doing as well as I was. It was a miracle, actually, that I wasn't paralyzed or brain damaged—and it was Rick who made that miracle possible.

However I recognized he was very, very worried and had realized how close he came to losing me forever, so I agreed to return to the hospital if my head hurt again, but I vowed to myself that I'd do everything possible to keep my head from hurting so I wouldn't have to return!

What was really worrying me was my vision. I was sure there was something else besides surgery to do to help drain the blood that had pooled in my eyes. It was impossible for me to read. I had always loved reading and studying. That was one way I passed the time when I wasn't working, but now every word I read was distorted or blurry because of the brownish-red "dead pixels." Even more frightening was that my perception of letters was all mixed up. I would see the letters, but they were wavy or in the wrong orientation, as if they were upside down or sideways. Or I would only see some of the words, not all of them. It was as if I woke up one day and was suddenly dyslexic, and had to solve every puzzle of a sentence just to read it.

I had never realized how much I took reading for granted until it was taken away from me. I could live without driving—in some ways, that eased my anxiety, in fact—but not being able to read was a cruel twist of fate that left me feeling shattered. I was certain there was a cure and I did Qi Gong eye work daily.

Fortunately, I have been blessed with many wonderful friends, and as soon as my friends learned that my eyesight was still severely damaged, they began taking turns dropping by and reading to me for hours at a time. The sound of their soothing voices and the images from the pages they read brought me great peace, and I soon spent most of my day sleeping, resting, and being read to from the piles of books I had stacked beside the sofa and my bed.

I really relished that period of recovery, but after about six weeks, I started going stir crazy. I hadn't been away from my work for that long *ever* and I realized that running energy through my body by working might facilitate my healing. After all, I reasoned, maybe I couldn't see too well, but my hands still worked. I would just let my hands and inner knowing take over.

So I decided to call up some clients to make a few appointments. I was confident I *could* work. My sight was damaged, but my hands were alive with energy! They would guide me.

She Walks with
Her Ancestors

I am traveling east with some women.
We stop at a seaside village where there is
a shrine. We run barefoot towards the sea.
It is warm and sunny. We follow a creek
through a small opening in between
some boulders to reach the expansive sea.
The waves are smooth coils. I see a huge
sea serpent beyond the waves. There is
no danger, just mythical beauty.

DREAM JOURNAL ENTRY

AMONG THE MESSAGES left on my answering machine was one from a client I had known for about fifteen years. She was a psychotherapist who used to be a bodyworker and would come by about once a month for a routine rebalancing.

"Whenever you're ready to work, I want to come in," her message said, and I decided she'd make a good test treatment since she'd known me for so long. When I called her and told her what had been going on, she was very concerned and supportive. She was also very eager to see me again—she trusted my hands.

I really had no idea if I was ready to work or not, and I was a bit nervous at the prospect. So I said to her, "Why don't you come over and we'll see if I can work?" She was open to that idea, so we made an appointment.

This was a real turning point for me. Ever since the aneurysm I had been tormented by thoughts that even if I were healed, I might never be able to work again. I kept these thoughts to myself, but they gnawed at me. If I couldn't do bodywork, what else could I do with my life? Obviously I wasn't dead or disabled in a wheel chair or anything like that. I could walk around, I could talk, I could use my arms, I could sense things. But a brain injury takes years to fully stabilize or heal so I really had no idea what might happen when I tried to coordinate my senses and hands so that I could work with another person.

"Okay, we'll give this a try," I told her, "but I want you to promise to tell me if my work is more disorganized than before!"

"I promise," she said, as she lay on the table. I placed my hands on her cranium and closed my eyes, letting my hands take over. When the session was complete, she got off the table and said, "Your work feels just like before!"

So that was my encouragement to go ahead, the nudge that I needed to tell me I was ready to go back to work. I knew if I was working I would have a life purpose; I'd be able to move my energy in a way that could help me renew myself while helping others. I knew that if I survived this brain trauma that I was meant to help people and to learn from this experience. But to reach that point, I had to have clients. So I got on the phone and started calling them up.

I started by seeing just two people a day, scheduling one for the morning and one for the afternoon. That was enough for awhile, and slowly things began to get busier until I was back in the swing of things, at least professionally.

There was still a ways to go before I was fully recovered. I noticed that I was having difficulty with my short term memory. In particular, if I was asked an open-ended question, I wouldn't remember a recent event unless a few details or prompts were included in the question. I was also extremely fatigued and sensitive to light and sound. I could feel my brain get tired in the same way a leg muscle gets fatigued with overuse.

And I talked constantly! I began to babble uncontrollably, the words pouring out of me as if they'd been stopped up for ages, driving Rick up the wall sometimes! I didn't quite understand why I did it, but it felt as if the words were leaping from my brain to my tongue and into the air with a will of their own.

Yet perhaps the biggest concern was my eyes. My eyesight was still causing me problems. The "dead pixels" had pretty much faded, but I continued to have trouble merging letters and numbers which were often scrambled. I got large-print books to read and my vision slowly began to improve until I was able to read regular print. Just as Moshé Feldenkrais had learned to speak again after his stroke by doing tongue exercises, I did ATM lessons and Qi Gong meditation and movements. Eventually, my brain started compensating for the distorted letters and words, filling in the blanks and rearranging the lettering to conform to what my mind knew the word should be. When it came to certain numbers and letters, I was still having trouble, I couldn't figure out the distorted image of the symbols. I was was patient with the healing process. I added acupuncture to my routine to help the eyes and Gerda Alexander's skin brushing to stimulate my lymph flow and blood circulation.

Driving was another problem. I could not read road signs properly but well enough to get around familiar territory. I wasn't supposed to drive at all at first, but one day I got in the car with a friend when Rick was away, and we took off like a couple of teenagers on a joy ride! That felt thrilling, to be so liberated and free! I knew I had a problem when it came to reading unfamiliar road signs, and it didn't seem to be improving.

Every two months I went to see the retinal specialist at the hospital for my follow-up visits, and that's when I got the news.

"Okay, here's what's going on with your eyes," he said. "Some of it will get better, but there's been permanent damage to the retina. The distortions are not going to go away. That's a permanent disability."

Permanent damage. It sounded, well, so *permanent*. But I wasn't accepting a label of permanence. They could call it whatever they wanted, but I knew that everything changes and so I hoped for my eyes to heal. If anything, the aneurysm had enhanced some of my abilities, and provided me a greater awareness of how suddenly our health –even our life—can vanish... or improve. It had provided me greater compassion for the health problems my clients suffered. I left the eye clinic in a state of acceptance and with a keener understanding of the trail the aneurysm had left in my body and psyche.

While I was at the hospital where the eye clinic was located, I decided to stop by and see my neurosurgeon. When I'd left the hospital I had asked for my records so I could review them to get a better understanding of what had happened and what they'd done. Among the things they gave me was a DVD that contained photos of my brain, arteries and aneurysm. It was fascinating to look at photos of my own brain, but at the same time a bit unsettling because I had no idea what it was that I was seeing. So I thought the surgeon could help me to make sense of them.

I'd made an appointment with him earlier in the week, and I had also asked if he could bring a coil with him so I could see for myself what they'd put in my brain. I waited for him in his office, and when he arrived from that day's surgery, his hair was tousled and he was dressed in scrubs. He looked haggard and worried, and I could tell right away that he feared I had come to discuss some sort of problem.

I greeted him, smiling widely, and told him that the main reason I'd come was to thank him for saving my life.

"I feel truly great!" I said, genuinely thrilled to be feeling so good. "Thank you so much for all your amazing work!"

His worry faded and turned to joy. "Well that's something I rarely get to hear!" he said with a broad smile. Apparently, patients aren't in the habit of thanking the people who do their surgery, and it was clear that he was not only delighted to hear it, but also to see how remarkable my recovery had been. Few people, he told me, survive an aneurysm the way I had, with minor residual effects. He emphasized that the location of the aneurysm was good fortune, and that was why I had recovered so well.

He showed me the coil he'd brought along and I was surprised to see it looked like a tube with titanium yarn attached. He explained the method he'd used and as he spoke, I could tell that he was excited to have the opportunity to explain his artistry. We poured over the pictures on the DVD and he showed me how the coil was inserted up my femoral artery at the top of my thigh. He explained how they negotiated all the twists and turns of the arterial path with guidelines and a camera. By the time he had finished, I felt as if I'd just had a mini-course on neuro-anatomy—with my own body as the class exhibit!

—

As I recovered in the months to follow, I tried to make sense of what had happened and the miraculous outcome. To awaken and be told that I'd had brain surgery—but to feel perfectly fine as if I'd just lost some sleep and desperately needed to nap—was like a surreal dream. True, my eyes were red for months, and letters and numbers were scrambled and sometimes mashed together, but once I began studying about the type of aneurysm I'd had I realized that something amazing had happened. The angels or spirit or whoever is in the heavens must have wanted me to survive, because when I think back to all the many stages at which I could have died I can't believe I survived. If Rick hadn't been home, or hadn't acted as quickly as he had, I had a fifty percent chance of dying right then and there. If I hadn't lived near the top trauma center in the Northwest, would I have survived? I am not so sure. If I had survived, there was another twenty-five percent chance that I would have another aneurysm within a week, which didn't happen.

The location of the aneurysm was another blessing. If it had been just a fraction of an inch higher or lower, I might have died, been paralyzed, or suffered severe brain damage. But by a miracle, it was in the best possible location, and once the aneurysm had ruptured, it clotted quickly enough to cause minimal damage.

Then there was the surgery. Not only was I very fortunate that the coil method was suitable for my type of aneurysm, and that the surgery was a success, but there were no other complications. These could have included a heart attack, another stroke, hemorrhaging, paralysis—any number of events that could have changed my—and Rick's—lives forever. But by a miracle, I sat up in bed after surgery and howled with laughter to realize I was all in one, moveable, piece.

Had it not been for my many devoted friends and family, visiting me, giving me bodywork treatments, encouraging and nurturing me, I am not so sure my outcome would have been as good. Their love and support gave me the courage and belief in myself that I needed to recover.

Perhaps the greatest blessing of all was the fact that a calamity had struck and I was safe and alive, reflecting on it afterwards. One of the memories that returns to me is of looking up to the sky from my bed in the ICU shortly after surgery, both the Green Tara and White Tara images nearby bringing me a sense of calm and promise. All those years of anxiety, of fearing that something terrible might happen, were now seen in a very different light. Perhaps those panic attacks were my intuition speaking to me. I had a looming sense of danger, a foreboding that something terrible was going to happen. It was odd how paralyzing the fear had been, yet once the event had occurred, I felt great peace.

As I rested on my bed and gazed at the sky, I acknowledged the miracle of my life and health and pledged that I would return to my work. From somewhere deep inside me I felt that my survival had been linked to my purpose here on earth, and that this purpose was related to the therapeutic work I had been blessed to learn, practice and help others.

Recovery meant, however, coming to grips with some cold hard truths about myself. My brain had been permanently altered. I would tire easily and see letters, distant faces and birds in a distorted way. At least those are the most notable vision disturbances. My memory seemed less precise, like I could only access memories through different pathway from before. And I would, for most likely the rest of my life, take some pharmaceutical medicines.

Perhaps most frustrating of all was to watch as my body gradually turned into an old woman's body. The weeks of being bedridden at the hospital, followed by months of sleeping and lounging as I recovered at home, turned my body into something it had never been before. Ancient. My body began to feel old, as my bones stiffened and my waist thickened. My entire body grew heavier from the lack of movement and the side effects of so many medications that left me perpetually bloated. I was never very tall to begin with, so with every pound I gained I felt all the more weighted down. My energy plummeted and the more I slept, the more I wanted to sleep.

My legs grew heavier and thicker and were no longer recognizable. I felt as if I were gazing down upon someone else's legs, these pale, thick logs that now carried me could not possibly be *my* legs, could they?

My hair, once long, had been cut short because the constant sleep had left it matted. It had become dry and brittle, breaking off when I tried combing it. When I looked in the mirror I saw another person looking back—a heavier woman with short, brittle hair. That was not me. Who was she? Would she be the woman who looked back at me from inside my mirror every morning for the rest of my life, I wondered?

No, I decided. I had not yet recovered. My body wasn't yet fully renewed.

Crossing the
Great Waters: Redux

MONTHS HAD PASSED, and my practice had steadily picked up until I was as busy as I wanted to be. My recovery continued, but it was slow, slower than I imagined it would be. When I left the hospital, I was so grateful to be alive—and with no major damage—that I underestimated the severity of my injuries. True, I did not have to regain the ability to talk or walk or read. My recovery was never challenging and difficult in the same way for me as it was for so many others who suffer aneurysms or strokes. I wasn't disabled nor in a wheelchair, and I could talk, use my legs and arms with precision, and I felt calm and wise. Indeed, it was a miracle I was spared severe damage.

The damage to my brain had been very real however, and slowed my cognitive abilities in subtle but pervasive ways so that daily living became exhausting. Just reading a simple sentence sometimes required translating it from a confusion of symbols to a coherent thought. The translation was often subconscious, but it slowed my comprehension and demanded additional energy from my injured brain, leaving me very tired throughout the day.

Even more challenging was recovering from the near death experience. I had come face to face with my own mortality and had a very powerful lesson in how instantly our lives can change—and even end. I was laughing on the outside, but inside I was shaken. I had almost died,

I kept telling myself; I had come within literally a fraction of an inch of death or paralysis or severe brain damage. Had the aneurysm been just a quarter inch higher, I might never have regained consciousness once I fell to the floor calling for Rick to help.

Though I was recovering slowly, I was recovering. I was using the Feldenkrais Awareness Through Movement lessons and exercising by walking. I was leaving the house more and more and socializing daily. Most importantly, I was working. The more I worked, the more fully engaged I was becoming with the world. I had always been in tune with my clients, but having had such a devastating experience, I became much more aware and compassionate. My touch became more sensitive as I discovered I could feel greater cues from the body with every treatment. Whereas in the past I was very aware of anatomy and the fluids and tissues that lay beneath my hands, after the aneurysm I found that I was even more aware of the most subtle tensions,and structures in and beneath the skin of every client. In addition, I felt like I knew more about each client before they had told me anything. I was sensing more of their energy field than I had before the aneurysm. My hands, it seemed, had come alive in a way I'd never before thought possible, as if they had an awareness all their own, as if they'd developed a powerful ability to sense interior landscapes of the human body.

I discovered, to my surprise, that my hair looked good in the new and shorter style. I bought a few earrings to decorate my exposed ears and felt pleased when I saw how the new look suited me. I could not deny that my face looked older since the aneurysm, as if the trauma I had endured had etched itself onto my face. I was healing but dehydrated and aged. The changes I saw and felt became all the more confusing because I was trying to identify myself as someone familiar. I turned to my journals, recording my observations as if I were a scientist tracking every subtle change.

I try to balance the body's aging with the injury to my brain and find that the residue it has left is piled high and seems to speed the aging process. I try to move my body more often but I become so tired. I try to get well by gobbling vitamins, but the recovery takes so long. I am regaining my health slowly, ever so slowly, more slowly than one can imagine. After all, I am reminded: It was brain surgery! No small event. I am to go on living, slowly, without nervousness. It is so easy now to be calm. Even if I want to, I cannot hurry. This is recovery time- But perhaps I am fooling myself. Perhaps I will always be like this: old and injured.

Sometimes I would have a bad day, a day filled with the old ways of sleepiness, a foggy brain and currents of anxiety, and I realized how ill I had been before the aneurysm, yet no one told me what they saw back then. "Back then," during the time of the panic attacks, before the aneurysm. My life becomes divided in two, Before the Aneurysm, and After the Aneurysm. From the comfort of the After phase, I can see my former self more clearly; no longer feeling the panic simmering inside me. During the panic attack years, sometimes Rick would try to tell me I was not well, but I was so lost as to what to do and where to go that I didn't listen to him.

Now, I was listening. My brain and arteries had forced me to pay attention. With the peculiar clarity that comes from damage to the brain, I realized that I had been more damaged before the aneurysm. Something deep inside me had been damaged, so severely that it had been crippling my ability to even leave the house, and had nearly paralyzed me with fear and phobia. Now that the worst had happened—my brain had exploded and left me with a knot of titanium at the base of my brain, a tiny bird's nest of thin filaments to keep me living—now I was more at peace.

—

After the winter of rest and renewal, spring erupted and blossomed into summer and the rains finally let up, I was ready to test my new self in a way I would never have considered before the aneurysm. After my horrifying panic attack at the airport on the way to Indonesia—and that long, terrifying plane ride across the ocean—I told myself I would never do anything like that again. Even then, I feared leaving home, even if Rick were by my side as he had been in Mexico, I was reluctant to travel. Yet I still so wanted to see the world! The tension between my desire to see the world and my immense fear of leaving home had left me confused, unwilling to risk any more than I absolutely had to. As I recovered from the aneurysm, and began to leave the house one small walk at a time, I grew not only stronger, I grew braver. The more I left the house, the more I realized I *could* leave the house, and the more I realized that I could leave, the more I knew I *wanted to* leave. After all, I reasoned, what good had any of my fears ever really done for me? The greatest trauma of my life had not happened in Indonesia nor Mexico nor even on a road with a flat tire during a quick trip to the store. The greatest trauma of my life had happened inside my home, in the safety of my own bed, when the aneurysm burst as I lay sleeping.

—

With the realization that another calamity had struck and I had survived, I began to reassess my future life. I had followed my dream of becoming a bodyworker, and I had followed my dream of marrying a wonderful man. Now having found those dreams, I wondered if it made any sense at all to stop pursuing other life dreams. I thought about restricting my life so as not to lose any more of my health. I thought about what it meant to lose something or someone. Even with this calamity,

I had not lost Rick. I had not lost my practice, my friends, and my involvement in life. Remembering the words of my teacher, Lama Tsultrim, warning me not to be afraid of living, I made up my mind that I would fulfill another life dream. I would go to Japan.

Ever since I became involved in Zen Buddhism in the 1970's, I have felt very close to the Japanese arts and culture, and had dreamed of one day going to Japan. So when Catherine, a dear friend and colleague, who has Japanese ancestry, proposed I join her for a trip to her homeland, I was thrilled! This would be the trip of a lifetime, an opportunity to travel through an amazing country and see for myself the beautiful Buddhist artwork, architecture, and gardens. Her adult children, who I knew well, would be joining us, and we would be traveling with two other colleagues. With four skilled bodyworkers—all close friends, I felt very safe even though due to our differing schedules, I would have to meet them in Japan. That meant flying there alone.

The memories of the Indonesian trip and the intense anxiety I felt began to haunt me. Would crossing that same ocean again bring the anxiety rushing back? Had I truly become calm since the aneurysm, or was I merely holding the anxiety at bay? Traveling such a great distance all by myself was scary, but I was very determined to go. To further my comfort and confidence, I gathered up enough frequent flyer miles to fly business class. That would mean a lot of attention from the flight attendants and a bed so I could lie down. I was going to be very protective of my brain and body, but I was going to go. I knew all I had to do was get there and my dear friends would support me once I got there.

I booked a night flight, so that there wouldn't be so many people at the airport. That turned out to be wise, because the slow, quiet feel of the airport calmed my nerves. Rick accompanied me as far as he could, but things had changed a lot since my Indonesia trip. He couldn't accompany me to the gate due to the attack on the twin towers in New

York City—once I passed through security, I was on my own. Once on the plane, I was so cared for by flight attendants that I felt like a celebrity, and soon I grew very sleepy. I had a full horizontal bed in an alcove on the plane, and was able to close my eyes and fall asleep under a fluffy down comforter.

By the time I reached Japan, I was happy and refreshed. I hadn't had the slightest sensation of panic, and the realization that I'd travelled across a great ocean all by myself without one, made me more aware of how far I had come in my life renewal. Stepping off the plane was like stepping into a new life. Catherine was waiting for me at the airport, and she stayed by my side throughout the trip, helping me with the chaos of negotiating a foreign culture, and translating an incomprehensible language.

Kyoto proved to be a dream come true. We stayed in a hundred year old house and visited the nearby gardens and Buddhist temples and shrines and Samurai castles. We shopped in markets, ate wonderful food and drank many cups of tea. It felt like a traveling meditation retreat, and for all the stimulation and excitement, there was a serenity that permeated every moment. Happily, instead of feeling anxious and worried with each new adventure, I felt my heart singing. When my brain had exploded, I realized, I wasn't just given the gift of life—I was given the gift of a *new* life.

But I wouldn't be honest if I said that I felt *no* anxiety. I watched myself carefully to be sure I felt safe and secure. My brain was challenged daily with overstimulation as we rode the trains and jostled our way through tight crowds, spending long days visiting national treasures. Such activity would challenge anyone, particularly anyone with a recent brain injury, common symptoms being fatigue, sound and light sensitivity, and overwhelm. But with all the daily activities, rather than allowing the stresses to turn into panic, my new brain simply adjusted to them.

A few weeks later, we returned home. We booked a night in the hotel before departing to separate destinations. We had a wonderful last night recalling the highlights of our trip, and then, in the early morning hours before the others awoke, I slipped away to the airline gate, alone and unafraid.

It had been a glorious trip, and the return flight was as comforting and attentive as the flight to Japan had been. As the plane descended into Seattle, I thought back to the serpentine road I'd taken to arrive at my life's destinations. Each step of the way, I had followed my heart and my dreams had one by one come true.

Like the forceps pulling me from my mother's womb, the aneurysm had pulled me from my past and brought me into a new world. It had been terrifying, yes, but by walking through that terror, I emerged on the other side, more alive and aware.

I stepped off the plane in Seattle and followed the crowd to the baggage claim, where the only baggage I would carry home was the baggage I would hold in my hands, and not my head. I had done it! I had gone alone to the other side of the world. More importantly, I'd come back home, feeling more connected to the world.

As I descended the escalator, I saw Rick waiting for me near the baggage carrousel and I hurried to him. I fell into my husband's arms and knew, all those years of living in fear had not been wasted. I had been terrified by possibilities—all the possible things that could have happened to harm me. Yet it was possibility that gave my life meaning—the possibility of love kept my heart open after years of disappointment, making room for Rick in my life. The possibility of new ways of sensing, touching and moving the body opened my mind to alternative medicine, forging my life's career—and it later kept me open to western allopathic medicine when I needed it the most.

Fear had never been my foe, as I'd believed all those years. Fear had been my teacher all along, teaching me to be vigilant, aware and to be open to the infinite possibilities before me. All the terror that had come before had brought me to this perfect moment, I realized, as Rick rocked me in his arms.

Let the living begin, I thought as I held on to Rick, I'm ready to be born.

Epilogue

IT HAS BEEN nearly four years since the aneurysm. My life is so rich!
With the passage of my February birthday—a time which I formerly came
to dread for the birth anxiety it brought—not a whisper of worry touched
me. My traumatic birth memories are quiet now, and for that I am grateful.
There is no more whooshing in my ears like an ocean swallowing me alive,
no more sleeplessness or trembling. The panic attacks are, for now, gone.
I know that for the rest of my life, they will haunt me. They may return
at any moment, but for now, I am free. Should they return, I am better
prepared to recognize them for the intrusive tricksters that they are, and
give them far less space to take root and grow in my mind.

One early morning, and I pick up a book and begin to read. It is
Oliver Sacks' *The Mind's Eye*, written in his usual style of neurological
case narratives. I read the first case, and then begin the second, but I am
unable to finish it. I close the book and put it down. I am trembling. A
recognizable sensation that indicates trauma is surfacing. I stay present
with the sensation until my tissues relax a few moments later. Sacks is
writing of brain and eye trauma and the ingenious ways that people cope
with severe disabilities. Reading his case studies, I breathe easily as I realize all that could have happened to me had I not been spared, and I am
grateful for my fortune.

My body gives me comfort now, despite its age and many changes.
It has always guided me, protected me, and so many times excited me. I

trust the body's wisdom totally.

I can still feel the tension line in my tissues from my right upper thigh to the base of my brain, and I get monthly bodywork and acupuncture to rebalance my whole self. Since the coil was implanted, my body has a tendency to contract on the right side along the path of the insertion. I continue to do physical, emotional and energetic work for the arterial, brain and lymph systems as well as full body alignment work. During the sessions I feel the tissues soften. I know them as old friends from the movement and hands-on work I do and from the images I have studied in the anatomy books.

—

This life's winding path continues for me. I continue to study and work, play and do art, and remain connected to my friends and the world outside my home. I venture from my home each day, discovering new adventures. The outside world that once so terrified me, now belongs to me, and I to it. I do not fear leaving home, for wherever I find myself, I know that I am home inside my body. Every day brings renewal and possibility and joy.

Having lived and learned a complexity of experiences and teachings, my own skill as a bodywork practitioner has been incredibly enriched. Although I have now been working for over thirty years, my practice shifts as I shift, though one thing has remained steady: my work is grounded in CranioSacral Therapy, Visceral Manipulation, and Feldenkrais work. I continue to study many new ideas and techniques and integrate them into my practice for like technology, the science of bodywork is constantly evolving.

Does one ever stop studying and learning? I realize I know nothing about embryology, the beginning of the body's formation. Emilie Conrad teaches about it and so does Bonnie Bainbridge Cohen, another one of the great somatic pioneers, who arrives in Seattle to teach and inspire me with another perspective as I am completing this manuscript. In my journal I reflect deeply about the insides of the bodies I have seen:

> I have had the privilege to dissect a fresh brain, not embalmed. It is like a blob of miracle-jelly, like snakes coiled tightly together. It will decompose quickly so I carefully use the scalpel to cut a slice of the brain jello mold, after it blopped out of the skull into a lab tray, loosened from its attachments. It looks like a jello dessert from a cookbook. Some people eat brains, I revere them. It quickly melts into a sad blob on the dissection lab table. And to watch it dissolve stretches my mind to believe this blob once regulated the functions of a life. And having seen and touched arteries in the dissection lab from the donated bodies, I reflect on the miraculous work the surgeons performed for me by winding the coil inside my femoral artery up to my head. There are a lot of curvy roads to negotiate! Then they built a dam at the rupture and re-routed the streams of blood to the other side. And I still function quite well.

Because of my many teachers and experiences, my work has become my spiritual practice where I watch impermanence, assist others to alleviate their suffering and work on myself as a practitioner. All of the training and resources I have assimilated in the past thirty years have not only helped me to develop as a practitioner, but have fostered my own renewal and resilience in healing from the aneurysm. Although my clients leave my table thanking me for all that I have done for them, it is to them that I owe my gratitude, for they have been my greatest teachers.

—

My commitment to my work to help others has never faltered, and in fact, has grown greater since suffering such a severe and terrifying injury. I especially want to caution you, dear reader, that becoming anxious does not mean you are developing an aneurysm. I cannot even say this connection was true for me. Trust your own body and find your own path to improved health.

I have learned that certain substances tire my brain and I cannot think clearly. When I eliminate these substances, my brain is clear. Most recently I eliminated gluten from my diet, and found the change remarkable. I am more energetic, my brain more alert, stiffness gone from my body. I have stopped blaming the aneurysm for all my health problems.

—

I cherish my friendships even more than before. I feel an intimacy with my closest friends that is precious. I make new friends with ease. And I find it easy to be friendly with everyone I encounter, from the barista making my espresso to the man at the gas station, taking my cash. The principles I have studied through bodywork and movement work and Buddhism now fall into place habitually. These are the habits I want to retain!

My creative life has been poured into this story so that others can learn from my experiences. I have learned to trust my body, to get to know my body and my mind, and I know that if you, my dear reader, do the same in whatever way that works for you, you will benefit.

My near-death experience did not involve a tunnel nor white light nor seeing loved ones on the other side. I cannot reach out to you, my reader, and tell you I have been to the other side and reveal to you what is waiting. I simply woke up and found I had been pulled back from the edge, with more calmness and appreciation for each day. It is my greatest wish that my story may give you a small flicker of insight to help you reach a similar place of calm, knowledge and strength on your life journey.

—

In closing, I offer you this prayer: May these words that I have set down in this memoir help you to find happiness and peace in your own life, and bring you comfort in knowing that with every breath you take, the pulse of all life moves through you.

ACKNOWLEDGMENTS

THIS MEMOIR WAS written to acknowledge all I have learned in these six decades from many of my teachers, both formally and informally; and to all those who helped me along the way.

Immense gratitude to the innovative teachings of Don Hanlon Johnson, Ph.D., John Upledger, D.O., Jean-Pierre Barral, DO, and Moshé Feldenkrais, D.Sc.

John Upledger, especially, taught me more than I can ever recount. He gave me permission to be myself as a therapist, especially when I was assisting him. He often said that we were to take his tools and ideas and make them our own. The last time I saw him at a clinical symposium in San Francisco a few years ago in 2005, I knew it would probably be the last time I would see him, for he was becoming unwell. He saw me and shouted across the crowded room, "Hey, I remember you!! How the hell are ya?" And we chatted about our news. That was all I needed to feel like I could continue on my path with his blessing.

And I give my unending thanks to all the innovative women in the Somatics field of inquiry, especially to Gerda Alexander, Emilie Conrad, Charlotte Selver and Bonnie Bainbridge Cohen.

I am so grateful to all the teachers of the Dharma whose books I have read or have personally studied with, in particular to His Holiness the 14th Dalai Lama, Namkhai Norbu Rinpoche, Lama Tsultrim Allione, Joko Beck Sensei, and Reginald Ray, to name just a few.

And thanks to Gerie, Rosa, Becci, Lisa, Anne, Gregory, Sheila, Tanya, Chris and Dawn who helped me so much during the time of anxiety, reassuring me that I would not die from it. You were right, and your faith in me and your optimism gave the encouragement I needed to make it through those dark times.

In addition, special thanks to Cathy Adachi, Mary Gillis, Annie Stocker, Martha Hurwitz, Martha Russo, Jeff Haller, Fernando Vega, Judith Bradley, Sue Berlin, Alice Friedman, and to Ava and Ruby Smith, the little ones who taught me so much.

For invaluable assistance in production, thanks to Robin Pederson, Robert Williamson, Lynn Thompson, Catherine Haynes, Rebecca Parsons, the folks at Gorham Printing and to David Roche for help finding the title.

I am fortunate to have found Janice Harper, who collaborated with me in writing this book.

Love and thanks to all our family, friends and practitioners who helped us through those years, you know who you are.

And it is such a blessing to have Rick in my life!

If I left anyone out or made any errors, it was not intentional. After all, I live with a brain injury!

May all Beings be free of Suffering and have Happiness!

RECOMMENDED READING

Somatics

Alexander, Gerda
Eutony, Felix Morrow Pub., Great Neck, NY, 1985.

Brooks, Charles and Selver, Charlotte
Sensory Awareness, Ross-Erickson Pub, Santa Barbara, CA, 1974.

Cohen, Bonnie Bainbridge
Sensing, Feeling and Action, Contact Ed, Northhampton, MA,1993/2008.

Conrad, Emilie
Life on Land, N. Atlantic Books, Berkeley, 2007.

Grossinger, Richard
Planet Medicine, N. Atlantic Books, Berkeley, 1995.

Feldenkrais, Moshé
Awareness Through Movement, Harper Collins, NY, 1972.
The Elusive Obvious, Meta Pub, Cupertino, CA, 1981.

Johnson, Don Hanlon, PhD
Body, Beacon Press, Boston, MA, 1983.
Bone, Breath and Gesture, North Atlantic Books, Berkeley, CA, 1995.
Body, Spirit and Democracy, N. Atlantic, 1994.
Groundworks, N. Atlantic, 1997.

Buddhism

Allione, Tsultrim
   Feeding Your Demons, Little, Brown and Co., New York, 2008.
   Women of Wisdom, Penguin, New York, 1984.

Beck, Charlotte Joko
   Everyday Zen, Harper and Row, New York, 1989.

Norbu, Chogyal Namkhai
   The Crystal and the Way of Light, Snow Lion, Ithaca, NY, 2000.

Ray, Reginald, PhD
   Touching Enlightenment, Sounds True, Boulder, CO, 2008.

Science

Barral, Jean-Pierre, DO
   Trauma, with Alain Croibier, DO, Eastland Press, Seattle, 1999.
   Manual Thermal Diagnosis, Eastland Press, Seattle, 1996.
   Understanding the Messages of Your Body, N. Atlantic Books, 2007.

Batmanghelidj, F., MD
   You're Not Sick, You're Thirsty, Warner, New York, NY, 2003.

Doidge, Norman
   The Brain that Changes Itself, Penguin Books, New York, NY, 2007.

Hunt, Valerie
   The Infinite Mind, Malibu Publications, Malibu, CA, 1996.

Levine, Peter,
   Waking the Tiger, North Atlantic Books, Berkeley, CA 1997.
   In an Unspoken Voice, N. Atlantic Books, Berkeley, CA 2010.

McTaggart, Lynn
   The Field, Harper Collins, NY, 2002.

Pert, Candace
Molecules of Emotion, Scribner, New York, NY, 1997.

Rothschild, Babette
The Body Remembers, WW Norton & Co., New York, 2001.

Siegel, Daniel J.,MD
Mindsight, Random House, New York, NY, 2010.

Simon, Tami, ed.
Kundalini Rising, Sounds True, Inc., Boulder, CO, 2009.

Taylor, Jill Bolte
My Stroke of Insight, Viking , New York, 2006.

Upledger, John, DO
SER and Beyond, UI Pub, West Palm Beach, FLA, 1990.
Your Inner Physician and You, N. Atlantic Books, Berkeley, CA, 1997.
SER: Deciphering the Language of Life, N. Atlantic Books, Berkeley, 2002.
Lessons Out of School, N. Atlantic Books, Berkeley, CA, 2006.

Resources

JudithMarcus.biz
Barralinstitute.com
BodyMindCentering.com
ChiklyInstitute.org
ContinuumMovement.com
Dharmaocean.org
Feldenkrais.com
TaraMandala.org
Upledger.com